THE OFFICIAL

DOWNTON ABBEY
COCKTAIL
BOOK

FOREWORD BY JULIAN FELLOWES

weldon**owen**

TABLE *of* CONTENTS

Foreword by Julian Fellowes 9
Introduction 10

1

THE LIBRARY

Stirred Drinks & After-Dinner Drinks 12

2

THE GROUNDS

Refreshing Drinks 40

3

THE GREAT HALL

Party Drinks 72

4

THE DRAWING ROOM

Predinner Drinks & Hangover Helpers 106

5

THE VILLAGE

Everyday Drinks 130

FOREWORD

Cocktails were slow to make an appearance on *Downton Abbey* but make no mistake: the Crawleys love to drink. In season 1, Robert Crawley regularly enjoys Scotch, dinners begin and end with sherry and port, parties include alcoholic punches, and plenty of wine and Champagne is poured—but none of the Crawleys or their servants sips a cocktail. The fact is, drinking before dinner did not begin until the end of the First World War and so the steady creep of cocktails into *Downton Abbey* only starts in seasons 2 and 3, when Robert asks his mother, Violet, "Can I tempt you to one of these new cocktails?" At this point, fashionable members of London society were beginning their evenings with a cocktail, a custom Lady Rose implores Robert to adopt. She is an early enthusiast, and Lady Edith gladly raises a glass once she begins making regular trips to London. Happily for Lady Rose—and the rest of the family—over the course of the show's remaining seasons, cocktails make more than a cameo appearance; they are, in fact, a mainstay of the household's dining and entertaining protocol. Edith, in particular, as a young career woman and urbanite, drinks them a great deal, in her flat, in restaurants, and at Downton itself, where cocktails are well established by the final episode. It takes newcomer Henry Talbot, however, to introduce the cocktail shaker.

This lively compendium is a celebration of the best cocktails of the *Downton Abbey* era and beyond. It is replete with recipes, cocktail trivia, historical notes, and excerpts from the show, and I hope you will find there is much here to savour.

JULIAN FELLOWES

LONDON, MAY 2019

"THERE'S NEVER A DULL MOMENT IN THIS HOUSE"

Drinking is very important at Downton. At least three types of wine are served at every upstairs dinner, plus port for the gentlemen after it. There's alcoholic punch at parties, plenty of Champagne, and, as the years go by, the gradual adoption of the cocktail. Mixed drinks are first mentioned in season 2, and it takes until the last season for one of the family—in this case Henry Talbot—to wield a cocktail shaker, but they lurk in the background of many a party. Edith, in particular, who, after Gregson leaves her his flat, lives a more modern life than her sisters as a bachelorette, is a serial quaffer of Champagne, G&Ts, and cocktails at various venues across London. Rose, representing a slightly younger and cooler dynamic than most of the rest of the family, is also no stranger to cocktails, which are regarded as decidedly "fast" by most others.

Cocktails were essentially an American import, and it's no surprise that the Dowager Countess wages a private war against them. When the show opens, dinners are very Victorian in style, and the predinner cocktail is unknown. The half hour before dinner was termed by one writer of the time as the hostess's "greatest ordeal," as she waited, no drink in hand, to see if the dinner was going to be a success or not. By the last season, the Dowager Countess has been beaten, and cocktails of many different hues are a mainstay.

Wine, of which Violet definitely approves, was usually French or German on country house tables. Hock, Burgundy, and the wines of Bordeaux, especially claret, more generally all feature regularly in cellar lists, along with port and other fortified wines, such as Malaga, Madeira, sherry, and such dessert wines as Sauternes. Spirits were also drunk, especially whisky (always Scotch), Cognac, and Armagnac.

Downstairs, the major alcoholic drink was beer. In previous centuries, it had been included as part of a servant's allowance. It was also the most common drink served in pubs, which feature in *Downton* as meeting places, and Mr. Bates works in one for a while after his estranged wife, Vera, forces him to leave Downton Abbey. Upper servants sometimes consumed nub ends of wine, and cheap punches were made on special occasions. Ginger beer and mildly alcoholic "pick-me-ups" can be seen at the various fairs, and these were usually home brewed in rural areas, though commercial versions were widely available.

Naturally, coffee and tea were drunk more often than alcoholic drinks, and water more than either of them, especially downstairs. The rich tended to drink seltzer water instead, both for health reasons and because it wasn't associated with poverty (it was also a standard mixer for whiskey). Cordials made from fruit syrup or flavored vinegars were also still in use, especially various fruit "ades," notably lemonade but also orangeade. Pressed juices such as orange juice were rather rarer and, like cocktails, seen as suspiciously un-British.

ANNIE GRAY, *Food Historian*

GLASSWARE

COCKTAIL   COUPE   WINEGLASS   COLLINS   FLUTE   PINT   OLD FASHIONED   MUG   PUNCH BOWL

∽ 1 ∾
THE LIBRARY
Stirred Drinks &
After-Dinner Drinks

OLD FASHIONED

OLD PAL

MAKES **1 COCKTAIL**

In the early 1910s, Scottish-born barman Harry MacElhone was hired by the American-born owner of the New York Bar in Paris to run the operation. A dozen or so years later, he bought the place, renamed it Harry's New York Bar, and made it into a compulsory stop on the itinerary of every well-known American expatriate and international celebrity. MacElhone is credited with creating two interesting Negroni variations that are worth trying. From his 1922 book *ABC of Mixing Cocktails*, the Old Pal dials down the sweetness of a Negroni and kicks up the flavor by using an aged spirit. The cocktail is a great example of how different a cocktail can become with a couple of modifications.

For the second variation, see The Boulevardier on page 28.

1 fl oz (30 ml) rye whiskey or a high-rye Canadian whisky

1 fl oz (30 ml) dry vermouth

1 fl oz (30 ml) Campari

Orange twist, about the size of a thumb, for garnish

Combine all the ingredients in a mixing glass filled with ice and stir until well chilled, 20–30 seconds. Strain into a rocks glass over fresh ice. Express the orange zest over the drink and drop it into the glass.

GRIGG

Will you tell him, or shall I?

CARSON

His name is Charles Grigg. We worked together at one time.

GRIGG

Oh, I'm a little more than that, aren't I, Charlie? We're like brothers, him and me.

CARSON

We're not like brothers.

— SEASON 1, EPISODE 2 —

COUPE

THE CHEERFUL CHARLIES

MAKES **1 COCKTAIL**

This recipe, a *Downton*-inspired variation on the Old Pal (page 14), is like a great music hall act. It pairs up two different aged spirits for a more complex flavor, and two different liqueurs for less bitterness and more citrus—a combination to get you a standing ovation.

½ fl oz (15 ml) rye whiskey or high-rye Canadian whisky

½ fl oz (15 ml) Cognac

1 fl oz (30 ml) dry vermouth

½ fl oz (15 ml) orange liqueur

½ fl oz (15 ml) Campari

Combine all the ingredients in a mixing glass filled with ice and stir until well chilled, 20–30 seconds. Strain into a chilled coupe or cocktail glass.

COUPE

HANKY PANKY

MAKES **1 COCKTAIL**

This cocktail is unique, not just for its use of Fernet, the inky dark and bitter Italian digestif, but also because it was created by Ada "Coley" Coleman, the second-ever female bartender at The Savoy hotel's American Bar in London. She invented the Hanky Panky in the early 1900s for Sir Charles Hawtrey, who asked for something with "a bit of a punch in it." On tasting the cocktail, Hawtrey is reported to have exclaimed, "By Jove! That's the real hanky-panky!"

1½ fl oz (45 ml) gin
1½ fl oz (45 ml) sweet vermouth

2 dashes Fernet-Branca
Orange twist about the size of a thumb, for garnish

Combine the gin, vermouth, and Fernet in a mixing glass filled with ice and stir until well chilled, 20–30 seconds. Strain into a chilled coupe or cocktail glass. Express the orange zest over the drink and drop it into the glass.

— LIBATION NOTE —

The name of the drink most likely came from a simple nonsense rhyme. Such rhymes were a common part of popular culture of the 1920s. Other examples would be hotsy-totsy and the bee's knees, both of which were used to describe something excellent.

COUPE

MARIGOLD

MAKES **1 COCKTAIL**

This Lady Edith inspired variation of the Hanky Panky (page 18), named after her daughter, draws a connection between the pioneering spirit of the original cocktail's creator, Ada Coleman, and the determination of Edith to live as a self-sufficient, modern woman. The Cocchi Americano gives the drink a golden hue, and the addition of lavender bitters harmonizes the botanicals in the gin and Fernet into a springtime garden.

1½ fl oz (45 ml) gin
1½ fl oz (45 ml) Cocchi Americano
2 dashes Fernet-Branca

2 dashes lavender bitters
Orange twist about the size of a thumb, for garnish

Combine the gin, Cocchi Americano, Fernet, and bitters in a mixing glass filled with ice and stir until well chilled, 20–30 seconds. Strain into a chilled coupe or cocktail glass. Express the orange zest over the drink and drop it into the glass.

EDITH

It feels so wild to be out with a man, drinking and dining in a smart London restaurant. Can you imagine being allowed to do anything of the sort five years ago, never mind ten?

– SEASON 4, EPISODE 1 –

COCKTAIL

METROPOLE

MAKES **1 COCKTAIL**

The Hotel Metropole, which once stood at the corner of Forty-second and Broadway in New York City, was well known for its eccentric clientele of bookies and cabaret performers. Essentially a nineteenth-century Cognac martini, the dry, almost-saline Metropole house cocktail is an elegant way to enjoy an old book.

1½ fl oz (45 ml) Cognac

1½ fl oz (45 ml) dry vermouth

2 dashes Creole bitters, such as Peychaud's

Dash orange bitters

2 cherries, for garnish

Combine the Cognac, vermouth, and both bitters in a mixing glass filled with ice and stir until well chilled, 20–30 seconds. Strain into a chilled cocktail glass or coupe. Garnish with the cherries pieced together with a cocktail pick.

— LIBATION NOTE —

Swap out the dry vermouth for sweet vermouth and you have a bracing brandy drink for winter nights.

COLLINS

BOSOM CARESSER

MAKES **2 COCKTAILS**

The cocktails of the 1920s often have lurid and evocative names, including this example from the 1921 book *The Whole Art of Dining* by Jean Rey, who commented rather acerbically that "American drinks are nothing but an endless variety of concoctions and mixtures . . . most of them bearing whimsical names by which they are known in Yankee-land." He notes that although Bosom Caresser wasn't a bad name, "it would scarcely be safe in this country to call for such a beverage." Regardless of the name, this is a luxurious cocktail with a decided 1920s kick.

4 fl oz (120 ml) brandy

4 fl oz (120 ml) light cream (see note, page 111)

2 fl oz (60 ml) curaçao or other orange liqueur

1 fl oz (30 ml) raspberry syrup

1 egg yolk

2 orange twists, for garnish

Combine the brandy, cream, curaçao, raspberry syrup, and egg yolk in a shaker. Add ice, shake hard for 8–10 seconds, and strain into 2 collins glasses over ice. Express an orange zest over each drink and drop it into the glass.

— LIBATION NOTE —

The egg yolk adds a lovely texture but can be left out if preferred.

LONDON COCKTAIL

MAKES **1 COCKTAIL**

This characteristically heady cocktail is given a frisson of danger by the inclusion of both gin and absinthe, the latter banned in France in 1914 (and in many other countries around the same time). At this point, Absinthe in France was like gin in England in the seventeenth century: widely available, often of dubious quality, highly alcoholic, drunk mainly by the poor, and blamed for everything from epilepsy to murder. Also, just like gin, it originated as a medicine (gin was supposed to cure the plague, and absinthe was used to prevent malaria) and rapidly became popular as a way to get very drunk very quickly. The United Kingdom never banned it (though they had tried to stamp out gin two hundred years previously), so it was still available in London.

½ **barspoon orange bitters**
½ **barspoon simple syrup**
(see note, page 37)

½ **barspoon absinthe**
1 fl oz (30 ml) dry gin

Combine all the ingredients in a mixing glass and stir well. Serve in a cocktail or Nick & Nora glass.

COCKTAIL

SHERRY FLIP

MAKES **1 COCKTAIL**

A very old style of drink, flips call for a whole egg (sometimes just the yolk), creating a hearty, fortifying mixture that tastes much better than it sounds. Any of the dry sherries—fino, manzanilla, amontillado—work here.

2½ fl oz (75 ml) dry sherry
¾ fl oz (20 ml) simple syrup
(see note, page 37)

1 egg
Ground or freshly grated
nutmeg, for garnish

Combine the sherry, simple syrup, and egg in a shaker. Add ice, shake hard for 8–10 seconds, and strain into a chilled cocktail glass, wineglass, or coupe. Sprinkle with the nutmeg.

— LIBATION NOTE —

You can use a sweeter or heartier sherry here, such as an oloroso, for more intensity, but be sure to dial back the amount of simple syrup (or eliminate it entirely) if you use a cream sherry or anything sweetened.

THE BOULEVARDIER

MAKES **1 COCKTAIL**

Like the Old Pal (page 14), this is another Negroni variation from Harry MacElhone's 1927 book *Barflies and Cocktails*. It makes a nice, pleasantly bitter drink—perfect after dinner.

1 fl oz (30 ml) bourbon whiskey

1 fl oz (30 ml) sweet vermouth

1 oz (30 ml) Campari

Orange twist, for garnish

Combine all the ingredients in a mixing glass filled with ice and stir until well chilled, 20–30 seconds. Strain into a chilled cocktail glass. Express the orange zest over the drink and drop it into the glass.

— **LIBATION NOTE** —

Want to make a Negroni? Simply swap out the whiskey for gin. For a refreshing patio drink, use sparkling wine in place of the hard alcohol.

COUPE

JAPANESE COCKTAIL

MAKES **1 COCKTAIL**

This recipe is from the 1887 edition of Jerry Thomas's *The Bar-Tenders Guide* and is basically an Old Fashioned (page 146) in a cocktail glass instead of on the rocks. And no, there is nothing Japanese about the drink other than the name.

2 fl oz (60 ml) Cognac	3 dashes Angostura bitters
½ fl oz (15 ml) orgeat syrup	Lemon twist, for garnish

Combine the Cognac, orgeat syrup, and bitters in a mixing glass filled with ice and stir until well chilled, 20–30 seconds. Strain into a chilled coupe or cocktail glass. Express the lemon zest over the drink and drop it into the glass.

BALTIMORE EGGNOG

MAKES **1 COCKTAIL**

This easy and delicious eggnog, which is basically a flip (see page 27) with milk, requires no cooking and shows up in almost every cocktail book of the mid-1800s in one form or another by the same name. Some recipes require only shaking, but this version from Jerry Thomas's *The Bar-Tender's Guide* calls for separating the egg, beating the white, and then mixing the white into the beaten egg yolk–spirit mixture for a frothy and delightful nog.

1 egg, separated

1½ barspoons rich simple syrup (see note, page 37)

1½ fl oz (45 ml) Cognac brandy or Jamaican rum or a mixture of both

1½ barspoons Madeira or port

4 fl oz (120 ml) whole milk

Whole nutmeg, for garnish

In a small bowl, beat the egg white until stiff peaks form. Set aside.

Combine the egg yolk and simple syrup in a small bowl and beat until blended. Add the Cognac and Madeira and beat until blended. Add the milk and beat again. Finally, add the whipped egg white, beat just until combined, and transfer to a goblet or mug. Grate a little nutmeg on top.

— LIBATION NOTE —

The foam created by beating the egg white is worth the effort, but if you're feeling lazy, just shake all the ingredients in a shaker.

TUXEDO COCKTAIL Nº 2

MAKES **1 COCKTAIL**

This cocktail is basically a dry martini dressed up with the addition of maraschino liqueur and absinthe. A smart suit or dress can change the way we think of a person, and in that same way, those minor additions shift the cocktail toward elegant.

1½ fl oz (45 ml) Old Tom gin

1 fl oz (30 ml) dry vermouth

½ barspoon maraschino liqueur

¼ barspoon absinthe

2 dashes orange bitters

Cherry and lemon twist, for garnish

Combine the gin, vermouth, maraschino liqueur, absinthe, and bitters in a mixing glass filled with ice and stir until well chilled, 20–30 seconds. Strain into a chilled cocktail glass or coupe. Garnish with the cherry, putting it directly into the glass, and then express the lemon zest over the drink and drop it into the glass.

— LIBATION NOTE —

The small amount of absinthe makes a surprising difference to the flavor of the cocktail. Add a little more than the couple of dashes called for and the drink will take on a strong black licorice taste that will throw the drink off balance.

ISOBEL

We've asked Molesley to look at Matthew's old morning coat. He's confident he can make it fit.

BRANSON

That's very kind, ladies, but, you see, I don't approve of these costumes. I see them as the uniform of oppression, and I should be uncomfortable wearing them.

VIOLET

Are you quite finished?

BRANSON

I have.

VIOLET

Good. Please take off your coat.

— SEASON 3, EPISODE 1 —

MORNING COAT

MAKES **1 COCKTAIL**

Tom Branson's initiation to life upstairs in the Grantham household required some adjustments by both sides. The morning coat was the first step of many that changed Tom and family forever. In this variation on the Tuxedo Cocktail No. 2 (page 32), the dry vermouth gets replaced by Cocchi Americano, for a less herbal and more citrusy drink.

1½ fl oz (45 ml) Irish whiskey

1 fl oz (30 ml) Cocchi Americano or other Kina Lillet–style aperitif

½ barspoon maraschino liqueur

¼ barspoon absinthe

2 dashes orange bitters

Cherry and lemon twist, for garnish

Combine the whiskey, Cocchi Americano, maraschino liqueur, absinthe, and bitters in a mixing glass filled with ice and stir until well chilled, 20–30 seconds. Strain into a chilled cocktail glass or coupe. Garnish with the cherry, putting it directly into the glass, and then express the lemon zest over the drink and drop it into the glass.

— LIBATION NOTE —

If Tom Branson were making this drink, he'd be sure to use a whiskey made in the Republic of Ireland rather than one made in Northern Ireland. Flavorwise, the light blended style of whiskey from either location will work. Kina Lillet was a late-nineteenth-century French wine–based aperitif with quinine and other botanicals. It has been out of production since the mid-twentieth century. Cocchi Americano works best as a modern-day substitute, but Salers or Kina l'Avion d'Or can also be used.

IMPROVED
BRANDY COCKTAIL

MAKES **1 COCKTAIL**

In the late 1800s, absinthe started showing up in many drinks, including in old ones billed as improved versions. The spirit's long list of botanicals usually includes anise, which gives it a sensation of sweetness that helps round out cocktails without the addition of sugar.

2 fl oz (60 ml) Cognac

2 dashes Boker's or
Angostura bitters

½ barspoon maraschino liqueur

1 barspoon gum syrup

⅛ barspoon absinthe

Lemon twist, for garnish

Combine the Cognac, bitters, maraschino liqueur, gum syrup, and absinthe in a mixing glass filled with ice and stir until well chilled, 20–30 seconds. Strain into a chilled cocktail glass or coupe. Express the lemon zest over the drink and drop it into the glass.

— LIBATION NOTE —

Gum syrup is a rich simple syrup, which means it has a ratio of two parts sugar to one part water, with the addition of gum arabic. The gum arabic is an edible stabilizer and thickener, bestowing a velvety richness to cocktails.

COFFEE COCKTAIL

MAKES **1 COCKTAIL**

This recipe, which originally appeared in Alfred Suzanne's 1904 book *La Cuisine et pâtisserie anglaise et américaine*, is a great way to have your after-dinner drink and coffee at the same time. It also makes for a potent brunch drink—think of it as a creamy coffee julep.

2 fl oz (60 ml) brewed espresso, at room temperature

2 fl oz (60 ml) brandy

2 fl oz (60 ml) heavy cream

1½ barspoons simple syrup (see note)

6 barspoons crushed ice

Ground or freshly grated nutmeg, for garnish

Combine the espresso, brandy, cream, simple syrup, and crushed ice in a shaker and shake hard for 8–10 seconds. Pour the whole mixture, ice and all, into a collins glass and sprinkle with the nutmeg. Serve with a straw.

— LIBATION NOTE —

To make simple syrup, combine equal parts sugar and water in a saucepan and heat, stirring, until the sugar fully dissolves. For rich simple syrup, use two parts sugar to one part water. Simple syrup will keep for 3–4 weeks in a tightly lidded jar in the refrigerator; rich simple syrup, stored the same way, will keep for up to 4 months.

2

THE GROUNDS

Refreshing Drinks

LIBATION NOTE

The sweetness level of every brand of orange liqueur differs, as there is no established standard. Taste the cocktail before pouring it into the prepared glass and adjust as needed with more liqueur (or simple syrup).

COUPE

SIDECAR

MAKES **1 COCKTAIL**

This is one of those drinks whose origin and name are locked in disagreement, with many claiming it came from the Paris Ritz, and others that it came about when someone drove a motorcycle into a Paris bistro soon after World War I. Old recipes from such books as the 1927 edition of *Barflies and Cocktails* call for all three ingredients in equal proportions, which makes for a shockingly tart and sweet drink. This recipe uses the more modern proportions of a sour, but if you feel the need to taste the original, by all means try it.

Lemon wedge, for rimming
Sugar, for rimming
2 fl oz (60 ml) brandy

¾ fl oz (20 ml) orange liqueur
¾ fl oz (20 ml) fresh lemon juice

Run the lemon wedge along the rim of a chilled coupe or cocktail glass. Pour a small mound of sugar onto a flat saucer. Tip the glass so it is almost parallel to the plate and gently roll its dampened edge in the sugar to create a sugar-frosted rim.

Combine the brandy, orange liqueur, and lemon juice in a shaker. Add ice, shake hard for 8–10 seconds, and strain into the prepared glass.

COUPE

THE SUFFRAGETTE

MAKES **1 COCKTAIL**

The most progressive of the three sisters, Lady Sybil made choices that often shocked the family, from her support of women's right to vote to her work as a nurse during the war. But none surprised them as much as her love of Tom Branson, the chauffeur. This adaptation of the Sidecar (page 43) is on the sweeter side.

Lemon wedge, for rimming	**2 fl oz (60 ml) brandy**
Granulated or superfine sugar, for rimming	**¾ fl oz (20 ml) crème de cacao**
	¾ fl oz (20 ml) fresh lemon juice

Run the lemon wedge along the rim of a chilled coupe or cocktail glass. Pour a small mound of sugar onto a flat saucer. Tip the glass so it is almost parallel to the plate and gently roll its dampened edge in the sugar to create a sugar-frosted rim.

Combine the brandy, crème de cacao, and lemon juice in a shaker. Add ice, shake hard for 8–10 seconds, and strain into the prepared glass.

— LIBATION NOTE —

Use a good-quality crème de cacao, which will add a slight cocoa bitterness and real chocolate flavor.

BRANSON

The truth is, I'll stay in Downton until you want to run away with me.

SYBIL

Don't be ridiculous.

BRANSON

You're too scared to admit it but you're in love with me.

— SEASON 2, EPISODE 3 —

COLLINS

RASPBERRY GIN FIZZ

MAKES **1 COCKTAIL**

The fizz is a style of drink that utilizes the effervescence of club soda or seltzer water to give levity and refreshing qualities and includes siblings like the Ramos Gin Fizz (see right), Morning Glory Fizz (page 108), Gin Rickey (page 118), and countless other variations. This version gets dressed up with raspberry syrup, a popular addition in the late nineteenth century.

2 fl oz (60 ml) Old Tom gin

¾ fl oz (20 ml) fresh lime juice

¾ fl oz (20 ml) raspberry syrup

5–6 fl oz (150–180 ml) club soda, chilled

Lime wedge and raspberries, for garnish

Combine the gin, lime juice, and raspberry syrup in a shaker. Add ice, shake hard for 8–10 seconds, and strain into a chilled collins glass. Add the club soda and stir briefly, then add as many ice cubes as will fit without spilling. Garnish with the lime wedge and raspberries.

─ LIBATION NOTE ─

Popular in eighteenth-century England, Old Tom is a style of gin that is slightly sweet. It got its name from signs shaped like a black cat (an "old tom") displayed on pubs to signify the gin was served there.

RAMOS GIN FIZZ

MAKES **1 COCKTAIL**

Although this is the most famous fizz, it is actually not a true fizz because it departs from both the classic ingredients and construction method (see left). The secret of this drink, created in the late nineteenth century by New Orleans restaurateur Henry Ramos, lies in the shaking: a full three minutes. That's a long time, but some feel it is the only way to achieve the trademark silky mouthfeel. Feel free to shake it as long as you can.

2 fl oz (60 ml) gin	4 drops orange flower water
½ fl oz (15 ml) fresh lime juice	1 egg white
½ fl oz (15 ml) fresh lemon juice	1 fl oz (30 ml) light cream (see note, page 111)
½ fl oz (15 ml) simple syrup (see note, page 37)	2 fl oz (60 ml) club soda

Combine the gin, citrus juices, simple syrup, orange flower water, egg white, and cream in a shaker. Add ice and shake hard for 3 minutes— or for as long as you can. Strain into a chilled wineglass or collins glass. Add the club soda and stir briefly.

– LIBATION NOTE –

If you double strain the drink by pouring it through a tea strainer or small fine-mesh sieve on its way into the glass, you will get finer bubbles and better texture in the drink.

COCKTAIL

THE ABBEY

MAKES **1 COCKTAIL**

This recipe, which comes from *The Savoy Cocktail Book*, is a great cocktail for using gins with more unusual botanicals, like citrus or floral components, but it works perfectly fine with standard London Dry, too. Topping it with a float of Champagne wouldn't hurt if you are serving guests at brunch, or even dinner.

1½ fl oz (45 ml) gin

¾ fl oz (20 ml) Cocchi Americano

¾ fl oz (20 ml) fresh orange juice

Combine all the ingredients in a shaker. Add ice, shake hard for 8–10 seconds, and strain into a chilled cocktail glass or coupe.

COCKTAIL

DOWNTON HEIR

MAKES **1 COCKTAIL**

The sudden death of Robert's heir on the *Titanic* catapults Matthew from Manchester lawyer to reluctant heir to the title of earl and the Downton estate. Taking The Abbey cocktail (page 48) and twisting it to be a more elegant fifty-fifty gin martini seems an appropriate tribute.

1½ fl oz (45 ml) gin

¾ fl oz (20 ml) Cocchi Americano

¾ fl oz (20 ml) dry vermouth

Combine all the ingredients in a mixing glass filled with ice and stir until well chilled, 20–30 seconds. Strain into a chilled cocktail glass or coupe.

MATTHEW
I've got a job in Ripon. I've said I'll start tomorrow.

ROBERT
A job? You do know I mean to involve you in the running of the estate.

MATTHEW
Don't worry. There are plenty of hours in the day. And, of course, I'll have the weekend.

VIOLET
What is a weekend?

– SEASON 1, EPISODE 2 –

SUMMER CUP

MAKES **1 COCKTAIL**

Also called a Pimm's Cup, this marvellously refreshing long drink was created in the 1820s by Londoner James Pimm at his restaurant. Starting from traditional English fruit cups, which were a mix of fruit, juices, spirits, and sugar, Pimm concocted a gin-based tonic, flavored with fruit liqueurs and herbs, and began selling it commercially in 1859. The company eventually developed six varieties of Pimm's, each using a different spirit—gin, scotch, brandy, rum, vodka, rye whiskey—though most of them are no longer available.

2 fl oz (60 ml) Pimm's No. 1
4 fl oz (120 ml) ginger ale

Ribbon of cucumber and orange wheel (optional), for garnish

In an ice-filled collins glass, combine the Pimm's and ginger ale and stir to mix. Garnish with the cucumber ribbon and orange wheel (if using).

LIBATION NOTE

Summer cups can be decorated with as many kinds of fruit as you like, each adding color to the drink. To make something special, try layering the fruit: add some ice, then fruit, then more ice, and so on, until you end up with garnish strata.

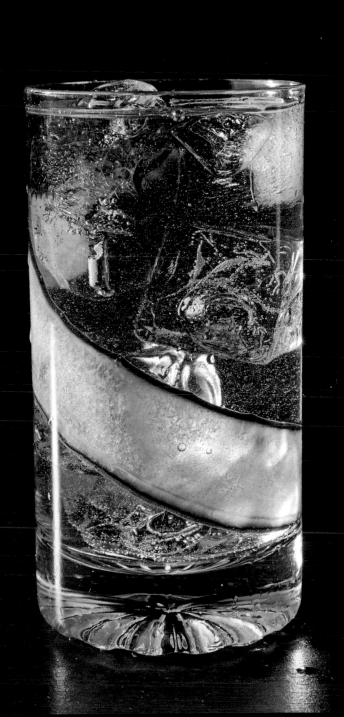

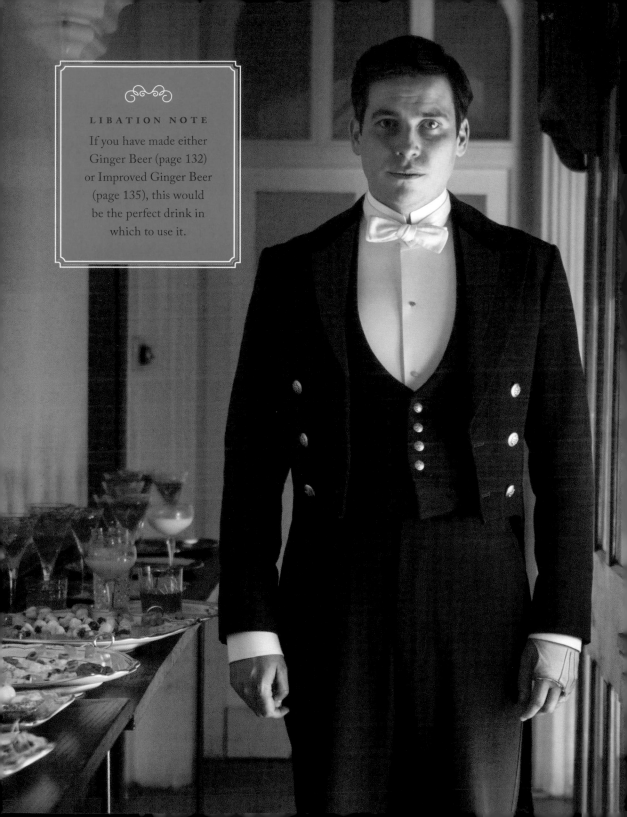

LIBATION NOTE

If you have made either
Ginger Beer (page 132)
or Improved Ginger Beer
(page 135), this would
be the perfect drink in
which to use it.

COLLINS

SUB-ROSA SUMMER

MAKES **1 COCKTAIL**

Replacing the mild ginger ale of the Summer Cup (page 52) with ginger beer adds the necessary bite that's as spicy as Barrow's wrath. Barrow would probably drink this alone, but we suggest you share it with a friend.

2 fl oz (60 ml) Pimm's No. 1
4 fl oz (120 ml) ginger beer

Ribbon of cucumber and orange wheel, for garnish
2 dashes Peychaud's bitters

In an ice-filled collins glass, combine the Pimm's and ginger beer and stir to mix. Garnish with the cucumber ribbon and orange wheel. Top with the bitters.

CROWBOROUGH
I remember this man. You served me when I dined with Lady Grantham in London.

THOMAS
I did, Your Grace.

CROWBOROUGH
Ah, there we are. We shall do very well together, won't we . . . ?

THOMAS
Thomas, Your Grace.

CROWBOROUGH
Thomas. Good.

— SEASON 1, EPISODE 1 —

COLLINS

GREEN SWIZZLE

MAKES **1 COCKTAIL**

Invented in the late 1800s, this Caribbean-born drink gets its name from the wooden tool that, when submerged in the drink and quickly spun back and forth between your palms, makes the drink frothy. If you don't have a swizzle stick, stir the drink with a barspoon and it will still taste good.

1½ fl oz (45 ml) white rum
¾ fl oz (20 ml) falernum
¾ fl oz (20 ml) fresh lime juice

1 barspoon absinthe
Dash Angostura bitters

Combine the rum, falernum, lime juice, and absinthe in a collins glass and fill halfway with crushed ice. Whip vigorously with a swizzle stick to combine. Add more crushed ice to fill and finish with the bitters on top for color. Serve with a straw.

— LIBATION NOTE —

The bitters will give you plenty of blood-red color on top, but the color of the drink itself will depend on your choice of absinthe, which can range from neon green (food coloring) to almost brown (natural color). Good-quality absinthe should be a nice vegetal brown.

COUPE

DAIQUIRI

MAKES **1 COCKTAIL**

Named for an area near the Cuban city of Santiago de Cuba, the daiquiri became popular after the recipe was introduced in 1909 at the Army and Navy Club in Washington, DC, by a junior medical officer, Lucius W. Johnson. Originally built in a collins glass and stirred, the daiquiri evolved into a shaken drink, but there's nothing wrong with having this over ice if the weather demands it.

2 fl oz (60 ml) white rum
¾ fl oz (20 ml) fresh lime juice

¾ fl oz (20 ml) simple syrup (see note, page 37)
Lime wheel, for garnish

Combine the rum, lime juice, and simple syrup in a shaker. Add ice, shake hard for 8–10 seconds, and strain into a chilled coupe or cocktail glass. Garnish with the lime wheel.

— LIBATION NOTE —

The daiquiri belongs to the family of mixed drinks known as sours or sour cocktails. Sours are some of the most popular libations, with a bloodline filled with such royalty as the Sidecar (page 43) and even the White Lady (page 103). You'd think that a recipe that calls for only three ingredients would be boring, but swap out the rum for tequila and you have a margarita, or trade it out for gin and you have a gimlet!

CLOVER CLUB

MAKES **1 COCKTAIL**

Developed by barman George Boldt, who owned Philadelphia's Bellevue-Stratford Hotel on South Broad Street, this frothy and delicate drink is named for a local men's club that met regularly at the hotel from the late 1800s to the early 1900s.

1 fl oz (30 ml) gin

1 fl oz (30 ml) dry vermouth

½ fl oz (15 ml) fresh lemon juice

½ fl oz (15 ml) egg white (about ½ egg white)

½ fl oz (15 ml) raspberry syrup

1½ barspoons simple syrup (see note, page 37)

Combine all the ingredients in a shaker and shake hard for 10–15 seconds so the egg white froths up and emulsifies. Fill the shaker with ice, re-cover, and shake hard for about 10 seconds longer. Strain into a chilled coupe glass.

— LIBATION NOTE —

Although this drink doesn't traditionally come with more than its frothy head as a garnish, try it with a mint sprig, slapped between your hands in a clapping motion to release the aroma before dropping it into the glass.

OLD FASHIONED

MINT JULEP

MAKES **1 COCKTAIL**

Basically a whiskey sling (a drink with spirits, sugar, and water) with crushed ice instead of water, this is the drink that launched mixology. Simple, elegant, and, most importantly, cold, it comes with an aromatic mint garnish that one inhales as one sips the sweetened bourbon.

¾ fl oz (20 ml) simple syrup (see note, page 37)

2 fl oz (60 ml) bourbon whiskey
3 large mint sprigs, for garnish

Pour the simple syrup into a julep cup or old fashioned glass filled with crushed ice. Stir well. Add the bourbon and stir until a film of ice forms on the exterior of the cup. Garnish with the mint sprigs.

— LIBATION NOTE —

Juleps can be made with spirits other than bourbon. In fact, peach brandy was the earlier basis for the drink, but your favorite spirit—gin, Cognac, and even fortified wines like sherry and port—will work here, too.

COLLINS

JOHN COLLINS

MAKES **1 COCKTAIL**

Legend has it that this drink was named for a waiter named John Collins, who worked at a London restaurant called Limmer's. It was first recorded in cocktail books in the late nineteenth century, and some early recipes called for whiskey rather than gin.

2 fl oz (60 ml) genever

½ fl oz (15 ml) fresh lemon juice

½ fl oz (15 ml) simple syrup
(see note, page 37)

5–6 fl oz (150–180 ml) club soda

Lemon wedge, for garnish

Combine the genever, lemon juice, and simple syrup in a shaker. Add ice, shake hard for 8–10 seconds, and strain into a collins glass filled with ice. Pour in the club soda and stir briefly. Garnish with the lemon wedge.

— LIBATION NOTE —

Genever is an old Dutch-style gin that inspired English adaptations like Old Tom, London Dry, and Plymouth. It is traditionally distilled from a mixture of botanicals that include juniper, and it is sweetened with a malt wine. The taste is something of a mix between whiskey and gin, which gives drinks a lively fresh bread flavor. Using whiskey here isn't that big of a leap from genever.

COUPE

DAISY

MAKES **1 COCKTAIL**

A category of cocktail popular around the late 1800s, the daisy was simply a sour cocktail with the addition of a small amount of seltzer water. Not to be confused with a fizz, which features three to four times the amount of soda water, the daisy has just enough seltzer to let the drink bloom.

2 fl oz (60 ml) Cognac
½ fl oz (15 ml) fresh lemon juice
1 barspoon orange liqueur

1 barspoon gum syrup (see note, page 36)
About 1 fl oz (30 ml) seltzer water

Combine the Cognac, lemon juice, orange liqueur, and gum syrup in a shaker. Add ice, shake hard for 8–10 seconds, and strain into a chilled coupe or cocktail glass. Top with the seltzer.

— LIBATION NOTE —

A barspoon is equivalent to 1 teaspoon (5 ml), in case you don't have a standard one in your bar.

COUPE

MASON DAISY

MAKES **1 COCKTAIL**

A twist on the classic Daisy (page 63), this version swaps out the seltzer for cider, something that Mr. Mason makes on his farm. A few dashes of bitters for Daisy's crushes on Alfred and Thomas add a little spice to complement the ginger.

2 fl oz (60 ml) Cognac
½ fl oz (15 ml) fresh lemon juice
1 barspoon orange liqueur

**1 barspoon gum syrup
(see note, page 36)**
2 dashes Angostura bitters
**About 1 fl oz (30 ml) cider
or ginger beer**

Combine the Cognac, lemon juice, orange liqueur, gum syrup, and bitters in a shaker. Add ice, shake hard for 8–10 seconds, and strain into a chilled coupe or cocktail glass. Top with the ginger beer.

DAISY
I've never been special to anyone.

MASON
Except William.

DAISY
That's right. I were only ever special to William. I never thought of it like that before.

MASON
Well, now you're special to me.

— SEASON **2**, EPISODE **9** —

CHAMPAGNE COBBLER

MAKES **1 COCKTAIL**

Cobblers are a style of drink from the mid-1800s that were designed, like juleps (see Mint Julep, page 60), to cool you down in a hurry. But unlike juleps, the ice here isn't flaky and snowy. It is instead crushed to the size of small pebbles, or "cobbles."

½ fl oz (15 ml) rich simple syrup or gum syrup (see notes, pages 37 and 36, respectively)

Sparkling wine (preferably brut)

Lemon twist and orange twist, for garnish

Mixed seasonal berries or other fruit, for garnish

Pour the simple syrup into a julep cup or double old fashioned glass filled two-thirds full with pebble-size ice. Add the sparkling wine to the cup to fill. Express the citrus zests over the drink and drop them into the cup. Garnish with the berries. Serve with a straw.

— **LIBATION NOTE** —

You can swap out the rich simple syrup for raspberry syrup, which will accentuate the berry garnish but not dominate the drink.

COUPE

LAST WORD

MAKES **1 COCKTAIL**

This pre-Prohibition cocktail first developed at the Detroit Athletic Club is a bumblebee of the bar world: by all calculations, it shouldn't fly, yet it does. Balanced and herbal, but not too herbal; sweet enough to balance the lime juice, but not too sweet—it makes a great nightcap.

¾ fl oz (20 ml) gin

¾ fl oz (20 ml) maraschino liqueur

¾ fl oz (20 ml) green Chartreuse

¾ fl oz (20 ml) fresh lime juice

Lime wheel, for garnish

Combine the gin, maraschino liqueur, Chartreuse, and lime juice in a shaker. Add ice, shake hard for 8–10 seconds, and strain into a chilled coupe or cocktail glass. Garnish with the lime wheel.

VIOLET
*It makes me smile the way every year we drink
to the future whatever it may bring.*

ISOBEL
*Well what else could we drink to?
We're going forward to the future not back into the past.*

VIOLET
If only we had the choice.

— SEASON **6**, EPISODE **9** —

LIBATION NOTE

Crème de violet is a liqueur
version of violet candies,
with a floral sweetness that
turns this drink into a purple
and powerful potentate.

COUPE

FINAL SAY

MAKES **1 COCKTAIL**

Do not cross Violet, matriarch of the Crawley family, whose skill at disarming opponents and getting what she wants is supreme. Like the Dowager Countess of Grantham, do not underestimate this cocktail, a riff on the Last Word (page 68). It may read like drinking a floral arrangement, but it's both potent and balanced.

¾ fl oz (20 ml) gin
¾ fl oz (20 ml) maraschino liqueur

¾ fl oz (20 ml) crème de violet
¾ fl oz (20 ml) fresh lime juice
Lime wheel, for garnish

Combine the gin, maraschino liqueur, crème de violet, and lime juice in a shaker. Add ice, shake hard for 8–10 seconds, and strain into a chilled coupe or cocktail glass. Garnish with the lime wheel.

CORA
I wish I could remind your mother we're on the same side.

ROBERT
I doubt it—when it comes to sides Mother is a law unto herself.

– SEASON 6, EPISODE 2 –

3

THE GREAT HALL

Party Drinks

NEW YORK SOUR

MAKES **1 COCKTAIL**

Essentially a wine-topped whiskey daisy—the daisy being a sour topped with seltzer—the New York sour is an elegant drink that would work well with hors d'oeuvres. Note that claret is an old British term for red wines from Bordeaux, but any nice fruity red wine will work here.

2 fl oz (60 ml) whiskey

¾ fl oz (20 ml) simple syrup
(see note, page 37)

¾ fl oz (20 ml) fresh lemon juice

About ¾ fl oz (20 ml) seltzer water

About 1 fl oz (30 ml) claret

Combine the whiskey, simple syrup, and lemon juice in a shaker. Add ice, shake hard for 8–10 seconds, and strain into a chilled cocktail glass. Top with the seltzer, then float with the claret, poured carefully on the back of the spoon to create a red layer (see note).

— LIBATION NOTE —

The trick to floating—or layering—a liquor, wine, or other ingredient on top of a drink is easier than it looks, and all you need is a barspoon. Place the barspoon on the surface of the drink so the convex side sticks up, like a little metal island, then slowly pour the liquid onto the spoon. Because the claret in this sour is less dense than the cocktail, it will float as a separate layer.

COUPE

LADY'S MAID

MAKES **1 COCKTAIL**

In the series, Cora's lady's maids, Baxter and O'Brien, are polar opposites, and this drink plays on those personalities through the New York Sour (page 75): it can be made sweet or bitter.

2 fl oz (60 ml) whiskey

½ fl oz (15 ml) simple syrup (see note, page 37)

¾ fl oz (20 ml) fresh lemon juice

About ¾ fl oz (20 ml) seltzer water

½ fl oz (15 ml) ruby port for Baxter version, or Campari or other similar Italian-style aperitif liqueur, for O'Brien version

Combine the whiskey, simple syrup, and lemon juice in a shaker. Add ice, shake hard for 8–10 seconds, and strain into a chilled coupe or cocktail glass. Top with the seltzer, then float with the port, for a Baxter version, or with the Campari, for an O'Brien version (see note, page 75).

— LIBATION NOTE —

The floats aren't really floats here, as their sugar content will make them sink to the bottom of the drink, creating a layer that will make the drink either slightly sweeter (in the Baxter version) or more bitter (in the O'Brien).

PUNCH BOWL

TEA PUNCH

SERVES **6–8**

Hot punches like this one were winter drinks, served at balls and at holiday celebrations such as Christmas and New Year's. The original title of the recipe was *Punch au thé à l'anglaise*, pointing out, once again, the association of the English with black tea. It comes from Alfred Suzanne's 1904 book *La Cuisine et pâtisserie anglaise et américaine*, which was aimed at French chefs aspiring to work in the United Kingdom or the United States. It purported to contain all the recipes that each nation regarded as a necessity on its tables. It was an odd claim, since in the author's view there really was no need for any type of food that wasn't French. For an added flourish, hang orange peel strips over the edge of the punch bowl.

1⅓ cups (385 ml) aged rum
1⅓ cups (385 ml) brandy
¼ cup (50 g) sugar
Zest of ½ lemon, cut into strips

¼ teaspoon ground cinnamon, or ½ cinnamon stick
¼ teaspoon ground cloves, or 6 whole cloves
2¼ cups (525 ml) hot strong black tea
8 orange slices

Combine the rum, brandy, sugar, lemon zest, cinnamon, and cloves in a saucepan over medium-high heat and heat until just below boiling, stirring to dissolve the sugar. Pour the hot mixture into a heatproof punch bowl or other serving vessel. Add the hot tea and orange slices and stir briefly. Serve immediately in heatproof glasses, small mugs, or punch cups.

GHILLIES JUICE

MAKES **1 COCKTAIL**

So yes, this recipe is really for laughs and a riff on Tea Punch (page 79) in honor of Mr. Molesley. Interestingly enough, however, it is thought that it was the desire to create one glass of punch at a time for a customer that evolved into the modern-day cocktail. England mastered the punch bowl over centuries, but it was the availability of ice extracted from frozen ponds and various storage techniques that together ensured ice would be available year-round, allowing bartenders in the United States to popularize and evolve cocktails. Enterprising Europeans and ex-pat Americans imported the idea, opening up "American bars" across the continent that showcased American bartenders during Prohibition.

| 1 fl oz (30 ml) whiskey | 1 cup (240 ml) Tea Punch (page 79) |

Put on your dancing shoes and hide your car keys. Add the whiskey to the punch and drink. Dance wildly.

ROBERT
They do say there's a wild man inside all of us.

VIOLET
If only he would stay inside.

— SEASON 3, EPISODE 9 —

LIBATION NOTE

Be careful with the
number of these fortified
cups of punch you drink.
On second thought, maybe
you should stick to
Tea Punch.

WINEGLASS

BRANDY CRUSTA

MAKES **1 COCKTAIL**

Perfected in New Orleans in the 1850s, this drink was not known outside of the area until Jerry Thomas included it in his 1887 edition of *The Bar-Tender's Guide.* The look of the drink, with a coil of lemon zest nested in the glass and a rim frosted with sugar, made it as irresistible then as it is today.

Lemon wedge, for rimming, plus 1 lemon

Sugar, for rimming

2 fl oz (60 ml) brandy

½ barspoon orange liqueur

1 barspoon fresh lemon juice

1 barspoon gum syrup (see note, page 36)

2 dashes Angostura bitters or other aromatic bitters

Run the lemon wedge along the rim of a chilled wineglass or coupe. Pour a small mound of sugar onto a flat saucer. Tip the glass so it is almost parallel to the plate and gently roll its dampened edge in the sugar to create a sugar-frosted rim.

Using a vegetable peeler, cut the zest from the whole lemon in a continuous wide strip, coil the strip, and slip it into the prepared glass. It will uncoil to almost fill the glass. This is a horse's neck twist (see note, page 84). Set aside.

Combine the brandy, orange liqueur, lemon juice, gum syrup, and bitters in a shaker. Add ice, shake for 8–10 seconds, and strain into the prepared glass.

COUPE

TURKISH ATTACHÉ

MAKES **1 COCKTAIL**

No other scandal in the series threatens ruin for Lady Mary or looms quite as ominously as the death of Kemal Pamuk. And yet, no one else could have dealt with the scandal as elegantly as Mary. A variation on the Brandy Crusta (see left), this drink, like that scandal, will quietly disappear in your glass.

Lemon wedge, for rimming, plus 1 lemon

Sugar, for rimming

2 fl oz (60 ml) brandy

½ fl oz (15 ml) velvet falernum liqueur

¾ oz (20 ml) fresh lemon juice

1 barspoon passion fruit syrup

4 dashes Angostura or other aromatic bitters

Run the lemon wedge along the rim of a chilled coupe or wineglass. Pour a small mound of sugar onto a flat saucer. Tip the glass so it is almost parallel to the plate and gently roll its dampened edge in the sugar to create a sugar-frosted rim.

Using a vegetable peeler, cut the zest from the whole lemon in a continuous wide strip, coil the strip, and slip it into the prepared glass. It will uncoil to almost fill the interior—like a bedsheet. This is a horse's neck twist (see note, page 84).

Combine the brandy, velvet falernum, lemon juice, passion fruit syrup, and bitters in a shaker. Add ice, shake for 8–10 seconds, and strain into the prepared glass.

> — LIBATION NOTE —
>
> A surprising ingredient that shows up in a lot of old cocktail recipes, passion fruit syrup (or "pash") makes this drink both exotic and exciting.

LIBATION NOTE

To make a horse's neck twist, pick a lemon with a relatively thick rind so you don't crush the fruit as you remove the zest. A vegetable peeler usually works best, but a paring or canelle (channel) knife can also be used. Cut the zest from the whole lemon in a continuous long, wide strip. Coil the strip into a tight spiral and carefully slide it into the glass, where it will unwind, almost filling the interior.

TURKISH ATTACHÉ
see recipe, page 83

VIOLET

Oh, my dears. Is it really true? I can't believe it. Last night he looked
so well. Of course, it would happen to a foreigner. It's typical.

MARY

Don't be ridiculous.

VIOLET

I'm not being ridiculous. No Englishman would dream of dying in
someone else's house—especially somebody they didn't even know.

PRINCE OF WALES COCKTAIL

MAKES **1 COCKTAIL**

Although it shares the same name as the punch on page 102, this cocktail is reputed to have been invented by Prince Albert Edward himself. It comes from a 1901 book titled *The Private Life of King Edward VII*.

1½ fl oz (45 ml) rye whiskey or a high-rye Canadian whisky

1½ barspoons rich simple syrup (see note, page 37)

¼ barspoon maraschino liqueur

Dash Angostura bitters

Thumb-size chunk pineapple

1½ fl oz (45 ml) sparkling wine (preferably brut)

Lemon twist, for garnish

Combine the whiskey, simple syrup, maraschino liqueur, bitters, and pineapple in a shaker. Add ice, shake hard for 8–10 seconds, and strain into a chilled coupe or cocktail glass. Float the sparkling wine on top (see note, page 75). Express the lemon zest over the drink and drop it into the glass.

> — LIBATION NOTE —
>
> The chunk of pineapple will get smashed up during the shaking of the drink, so there's no need to muddle the fruit, but you will end up with a lot of pulp in your shaker. To make a drink fit for a prince, double strain it by pouring it through a tea strainer or small fine-mesh sieve on its way into the glass.

COUPE

WILD ROSE

MAKES **1 COCKTAIL**

Rebellious and fun-loving Lady Rose needs a cocktail that balances her wild and experimental side with her traditional one. This drink, based on the Prince of Wales Cocktail (page 87)—she danced with the prince at her debutante ball—calls for tequila, a spirit known but not common in 1920s England. It is a liquor from the Americas, where Rose moves to after marrying Atticus.

1½ fl oz (45 ml) reposado tequila

1½ barspoons rich simple syrup (see note, page 37)

¼ barspoon maraschino liqueur

Dash Angostura bitters

Thumb-size chunk pineapple

1½ fl oz (45 ml) sparkling wine (preferably brut)

Orange twist rose, for garnish (see note)

Combine the tequila, simple syrup, maraschino liqueur, bitters, and pineapple in a shaker. Add ice, shake hard for 8–10 seconds, and strain into a chilled coupe or cocktail glass. Float the sparkling wine on top (see note, page 75), then garnish with the orange twist rose.

— LIBATION NOTE —

An orange twist rose is pretty and easy to make: wind a medium-width but long strip of orange zest into itself and skewer it with a cocktail pick to keep it from unwinding.

ROSE

*Oh, by the way, Madeleine Allsopp asked if I'd go on to the Embassy
with some friends of hers, afterwards.*

ROBERT

Tonight? After the dinner?

CORA

Rose, once you get past Tuesday . . .

ROSE

*I don't think you have to be presented to go to the Embassy Club.
And I do love Ambrose and his orchestra. Please.*

MARY

Your niece is a flapper. Accept it.

ROSE

I'm not a flapper. But can I go?

— SEASON 4, EPISODE 9 —

FLUTE

FRENCH 75

MAKES **1 COCKTAIL**

Created around the time of World War I, this elegant drink was said to pack the wallop of a 75mm French artillery shell, thus its name.

1½ fl oz (45 ml) gin	**3 dashes orange bitters**
½ fl oz (15 ml) fresh lemon juice	**2 lemon zest strips**
½ fl oz (15 ml) simple syrup (see note, page 37)	**About 2 fl oz (60 ml) brut sparkling wine, chilled**

Combine the gin, lemon juice, simple syrup, bitters, and 1 zest strip in a shaker. Add ice, shake hard for 8–10 seconds, and strain into a chilled champagne flute or coupe. Top with the sparkling wine. Express the remaining zest strip over the drink and drop it into the glass.

— LIBATION NOTE —

Shaking the lemon zest with the other ingredients can make the drink a little bitter, so if you want a bit less intensity, leave it out.

ARCHIE'S MEMORIAL

MAKES **1 COCKTAIL**

If Mrs. Patmore were a bartender, she would have created a drink to honor her nephew, Archie Philpotts, who died in the war but was left out of his town's memorial. This slight twist on a French 75 (page 91) gets the subtle but meaningful addition of sage leaves, which gives it a citrusy herbal hint.

1½ fl oz (45 ml) gin

½ fl oz (15 ml) fresh lemon juice

½ fl oz (15 ml) simple syrup
(see note, page 37)

2 dashes orange bitters

4 fresh sage leaves

About 2 fl oz (60 ml) brut
sparkling wine, chilled

Lemon twist, for garnish

Combine the gin, lemon juice, simple syrup, bitters, and sage leaves in a shaker. Add ice, shake hard for 8–10 seconds, and strain into a chilled champagne flute or coupe. Top with the sparkling wine. Express the lemon zest over the drink and drop it into the glass.

— LIBATION NOTE —

It wouldn't be a drink from Mrs. Patmore if it didn't include food. By design, this drink goes very well with a nice piece of Cheddar cheese.

FLUTE

KIR ROYAL

MAKES **1 COCKTAIL**

This iconic French cocktail was named for a certain Canon Félix Kir, once mayor of Dijon, France, a city that produces crème de cassis from local black currants.

5 fl oz (150 ml) Champagne or sparkling wine, chilled

2 barspoons crème de cassis

Lemon twist, for garnish

Pour the Champagne and cassis into a chilled champagne flute and stir briefly. Express the lemon zest over the drink and drop it into the glass.

— LIBATION NOTE —

Making a drink royal simply means that sparkling wine has been added to it. It works with any drink that could use a little lengthening or in which soda water is used.

STIRRUP CUP

SERVES **6**

At Downton, elegantly dressed ladies and gentlemen regularly romped through the countryside in pursuit of a fox before settling down to a hearty tea. Hunting tradition held that once the riders and hounds were all assembled at the meet, a drink would be handed round to send them on their way. Often it was just a simple drink of port. This cup, which comes from Henry Craddock's *The Savoy Cocktail Book* and was originally made with claret, veers dangerously into proper cocktail territory.

1¼ cups (10 fl oz/300 ml) ruby port

2½ fl oz (75 ml) maraschino liqueur

2½ fl oz (75 ml) curaçao

1½ barspoons superfine sugar

2½ cups (20 fl oz/600 ml) soda water, chilled

1 orange, thinly sliced in half wheels

6 pineapple rounds, peeled, and cut into eighths

½ cucumber, thinly sliced into wheels

Fresh mint sprigs, for garnish

Combine the port, maraschino liqueur, curaçao, and sugar in a punch bowl and stir until the sugar dissolves. Pour in the soda water and stir, then add ice and stir again. Add the orange, pineapple, and cucumber slices. Serve in cups, making sure to include some cucumber, orange, and pineapple in each cup. Garnish each cup with mint.

COUPE

THE BOOTHBY

MAKES **1 COCKTAIL**

This variation on a Manhattan (page 147) strikes the right balance between sweet and bitter, and it lends a nice effervescence and sophistication worthy of a cocktail party. The recipe was developed by William "Cocktail Bill" Boothby, a bartender and author who tended bar at the Palace Hotel in San Francisco in the years just before the earthquake of 1906 reduced much of the city to ruins.

1½ fl oz (45 ml) rye whiskey or a high-rye Canadian whisky

1½ fl oz (45 ml) sweet vermouth

2 dashes Angostura bitters

1 fl oz (30 ml) sparkling wine (preferably brut), chilled

Combine the whiskey, vermouth, and bitters in a mixing glass filled with ice and stir until well chilled, 20–30 seconds. Strain into a chilled coupe or cocktail glass. Float the sparkling wine on top (see note, page 75).

— LIBATION NOTE —

To ensure the bubbles stay bubbly in the drink, make sure the sparkling wine and the cocktail are as cold as possible. Carbonation goes flat when the liquids are warm.

PINEAPPLE JULEP

PUNCH BOWL

SERVES **4**

Despite the "julep" in the name, this drink has nothing in common with other similarly named drinks, such as the Mint Julep on page 60, but is instead a punch. A recipe for it appears in William Terrington's 1869 *Cooling Cups and Dainty Drinks*, which was the earliest British book to include recipes for cocktails as well as other popular British and European libations.

1 pineapple, peeled and chopped

4 fl oz (120 ml) Bols barrel-aged genever

4 fl oz (120 ml) maraschino liqueur

4 fl oz (120 ml) raspberry syrup

Juice of 2 oranges

1 bottle (750 ml) sparkling wine, chilled

About 3⅓ cups (450 g) shaved or crushed ice

Seasonal berries, for garnish

Combine the pineapple, genever, maraschino liqueur, raspberry syrup, orange juice, wine, and ice in a punch bowl and stir to combine. Garnish with the berries. To serve, ladle into punch cups.

— LIBATION NOTE —

If you can't find barrel-aged genever, feel free to substitute your favorite whiskey here.

PLANTER'S PUNCH

MAKES **1 COCKTAIL**

This Jamaican drink seems to have inspired a legion to concoct the beverage. But oddly, there is no agreement on what the original recipe was, other than something vaguely tropical with citrus and rum. No two recipes are alike.

2 fl oz (60 ml) dark rum

2 fl oz (60 ml) fresh grapefruit juice

1 fl oz (30 ml) pineapple juice

1 fl oz (30 ml) fresh lime juice

½ fl oz (15 ml) simple syrup (see note, page 37)

1 fl oz (30 ml) club soda

Pineapple spear, for garnish

Combine the rum, fruit juices, and simple syrup in a shaker. Add ice, shake hard for 8–10 seconds, and strain into a collins glass filled with ice. Pour in the club soda and stir briefly. Garnish with the pineapple spear.

— LIBATION NOTE —

Some recipes call for orange juice instead of grapefruit, lime juice instead of lemon, with grenadine as an additional sweetener. Feel free to experiment and find your own tropical escape.

FISH HOUSE PUNCH

SERVES **15–17**

This once-secret recipe was invented in 1732 at Philadelphia's venerable Fish House Club, which counted George Washington as a member. The drink packs a wallop, so make sure to sip slowly and to let the ice block dilute the punch.

2 bottles (750 ml each) dark rum

2¼ cups (525 ml) brandy

1 cup (240 ml) peach brandy

1¼ cups (300 ml) fresh lime juice

1¼ cups (300 ml) fresh lemon juice

1 cup (240 ml) simple syrup (see note, page 37)

¼ cup (60 ml) water

1 large ice block, for serving

Lemon and lime slices, for garnish

Pour the rum, both brandies, the citrus juices, the simple syrup, and the water into a large container made of stainless steel or other nonreactive material. Stir well, cover, and refrigerate until well chilled, at least 4 hours.

Place the ice block in the center of a large punch bowl, then pour in the punch and garnish with the citrus slices. Ladle into punch cups.

— LIBATION NOTE —

Peach brandy and peach liqueur are very different spirits, so be sure to get the unsweetened brandy, or cut the simple syrup amount in half if you can find only the liqueur.

PRINCE OF WALES PUNCH

SERVES **10**

Paying homage to the royal family was a tried-and-tested way to make a recipe sound suitably upmarket. The Prince of Wales is the title given to the (male) heir to the throne, who at the time of *Downton* was Edward, later Edward VIII, notable for his good looks, dapper dress sense, and many love affairs, often with married women. He appears briefly in *Downton* and is the reason for Lady Mary's brief career as a burglar, when she tries to retrieve one of his love letters, stolen from Freda Dudley Ward by the thoroughly villainous Terence Sampson during a party in London. This punch is light, refreshing, and ideal for those who don't like sweet cocktails. The very real Freda Dudley Ward was, like the fictional *Downton* daughters, born to an English father and American heiress mother. She was the prince's lover from 1918 until he fell in love with Wallis Simpson in 1934. Her husband divorced her on grounds of adultery in 1931.

1¾ cups (425 ml) Champagne

1¾ cups (425 ml) hock or other light Rhenish-style wine

2 fl oz (60 ml) brandy

2 fl oz (60 ml) curaçao

2 fl oz (60 ml) raspberry syrup

1 fl oz (30 ml) rum

Juice of ½ lemon

Juice of ½ orange

3½ cups (825 ml) soda water, chilled

Combine all the ingredients in a large container made of stainless steel or other nonreactive material, stir well, and serve in punch cups over ice.

COUPE

WHITE LADY

MAKES **1 COCKTAIL**

So famous was this drink at the American Bar at The Savoy in London that a cocktail shaker that held a White Lady was buried within the walls of the bar during a renovation in 1927.

2 fl oz (60 ml) gin
¾ fl oz (20 ml) fresh lemon juice

½ fl oz (15 ml) orange liqueur
1½ barspoons gum syrup (see note, page 36)

Combine all the ingredients in a shaker. Add ice, shake hard for 8–10 seconds, and strain into a chilled coupe or cocktail glass.

— **LIBATION NOTE** —

There are times when swapping out the simple syrup for liqueur sounds easier, but beware: Orange liqueurs are usually 80 proof, and increasing the amount to bump up the sweetness also adds alcohol. That minor addition can throw the drink off balance.

COCKTAIL

WEDDING COAT

MAKES **1 COCKTAIL**

Kindhearted, ethical, and efficient Mrs. Hughes always made sure the downstairs ran as smoothly as this cocktail. Based on the White Lady (page 103), the crème de cassis imbues the drink with floral and fruity notes that contrast nicely with the gin and gives it a lovely purple color.

2 fl oz (60 ml) gin

¾ fl oz (20 ml) fresh lemon juice

½ fl oz (15 ml) crème de cassis

1½ barspoons gum syrup (see note, page 36)

Combine all the ingredients in a shaker. Add ice, shake hard for 8–10 seconds, and strain into a chilled cocktail glass or coupe.

— LIBATION NOTE —

Much as with any piece of clothing, texture makes all the difference, and here the gum syrup turns this cocktail from a simple gin sour into a velvety classic, worthy of the finest celebration.

CARSON

But if I get my trousers wet?

MRS. HUGHES

If you get them wet, we'll dry them.

CARSON

Suppose I fall over?

MRS. HUGHES

Suppose a bomb goes off? Suppose we're hit by a falling star?
You can hold my hand. Then we'll both go in together.

CARSON

I think I will hold your hand. It'll make me feel a bit steadier.

— SEASON 4, EPISODE 9 —

4

THE DRAWING ROOM

Predinner Drinks
& Hangover Helpers

MORNING GLORY FIZZ

MAKES **1 COCKTAIL**

This hangover remedy from the late nineteenth century is unique in its use of Scotch whisky, with the club soda designed both to settle the stomach and to provide lift to the drink. The nutmeg, preferably freshly grated, makes a big difference to the drink, so don't leave it out.

2 fl oz (60 ml) Scotch whisky

½ fl oz (15 ml) crème de cacao

**1 fl oz (30 ml) light cream
(see note, page 111)**

4 fl oz (120 ml) club soda

Ground or freshly grated nutmeg, for garnish

Combine the whisky, crème de cacao, and cream in a shaker. Add ice, shake hard for 8–10 seconds, and strain into a collins glass or a double old fashioned glass over ice. Add the club soda and stir well. Sprinkle with the nutmeg.

LIBATION NOTE

This drink is very dry and refreshing, so if you would like it a touch sweeter, double the amount of crème de cacao.

BATES

Do you never doubt, for just one minute? I wouldn't blame you.

ANNA

No, and before you ask, I don't doubt that the sun will rise in the east, either.

— SEASON 3, EPISODE 1 —

COLLINS

NEVER DOUBT

MAKES **1 COCKTAIL**

There is no other relationship on *Downton Abbey* that withstands as many challenges as the one between Anna and John Bates. Despite Barrow's scheming, prison time for each of them, and the vindictive Vera, the pair manage to never doubt. This cocktail, which is based on the Morning Glory Fizz (page 108), honors that bond.

2 fl oz (60 ml) Cognac

1 fl oz (30 ml) orgeat syrup

1 fl oz (30 ml) light cream (see note)

4 fl oz (120 ml) club soda

Ground or freshly grated nutmeg, for garnish

Combine the Cognac, orgeat syrup, and cream in a shaker. Add ice, shake hard for 8–10 seconds, and strain into a collins glass over ice. Add the club soda and stir well. Sprinkle with the nutmeg.

― LIBATION NOTE ―

Half-and-half or a mixture of equal parts whole milk and heavy cream works well if you cannot find light cream.

COUPE

CORPSE REVIVER № 1

MAKES **1 COCKTAIL**

While there is nothing medicinal about this cocktail, despite its intended use to cure hangovers, there was plenty of medical drama when Downton Abbey housed a convalescence hospital for injured soldiers and Isobel Crawley helped out at the village hospital. This drink became popular when it was published in Harry Craddock's *The Savoy Cocktail Book* with this prescription: "To be taken before 11 a.m., or whenever steam and energy are needed."

1½ fl oz (45 ml) sweet vermouth

¾ fl oz (20 ml) Calvados or other apple brandy

¾ fl oz (20 ml) Cognac

Combine all the ingredients in a mixing glass filled with ice and stir until well chilled, 20–30 seconds. Strain into a chilled coupe or cocktail glass.

LADY ANSTRUTHER
No cocktails? I thought everyone had them now.

MARY
Not at Downton. Our butler tried them once and he hasn't recovered.

– SEASON **5**, EPISODE **1** –

CLARKSON'S ANTIDOTE

MAKES **1 COCKTAIL**

Among classic cocktail enthusiasts, the Corpse Reviver No. 1 (see left) is considered a bit lackluster. By spotlighting the apple brandy with an entourage of supporting flavors—cinnamon from the bitters, vanilla from the dark rum, anise from the absinthe—this *Downton* variation, created in honor of Dr. Clarkson, is a lifesaver.

1½ fl oz (45 ml) sweet vermouth

1 fl oz (30 ml) Calvados or other apple brandy

½ fl oz (15 ml) dark rum

¼ barspoon absinthe

2 dashes Angostura bitters

Combine all the ingredients in a mixing glass filled with ice and stir until well chilled, 20–30 seconds. Strain into a chilled coupe or cocktail glass.

ISOBEL
Will you really deny the man his chance of life?

CLARKSON
I just wish it was a treatment I was more familiar with.

ISOBEL
Will that serve as your excuse when he dies?

CLARKSON
Nurse! Will you prepare Mr. Drake for his procedure, please? Well, Mrs. Crawley, I have a feeling we will sink or swim together.

– SEASON 1, EPISODE 2 –

COUPE

CORPSE REVIVER № 2

MAKES **1 COCKTAIL**

The drinks in this macabre series have nothing in common except that all of them are strong cocktails and meant to cure hangovers. New York–born Crosby Gaige, a bon vivant of the 1930s, once said that one Corpse Reviver would revive any self-respecting corpse, but that four taken in swift succession would return the corpse to a reclining position.

¾ fl oz (20 ml) gin

¾ fl oz (20 ml) Cocchi Americano

¾ fl oz (20 ml) orange liqueur

¾ fl oz (20 ml) fresh lemon juice

2 dashes absinthe

Combine all the ingredients in a shaker. Add ice, shake hard for 8–10 seconds, and strain into a chilled coupe or cocktail glass.

— **LIBATION NOTE** —

If you can't find Cocchi Americano or don't enjoy the quinine bitterness of the aperitif wine, you can substitute Lillet Blanc.

COUPE

PETRICK

MAKES **1 COCKTAIL**

The appearance of Major Peter Gordon, the mysterious Princess Patricia's Canadian Light Infantry burn victim at the Downton Abbey convalescent hospital, generates questions that never have a chance to be answered. Is he Patrick Crawley, who everyone believed died on the *Titanic*, back from the dead? Or is he Peter Gordon, who worked with Patrick at the Foreign Office? This cocktail, a twist on the Corpse Reviver No. 2 (page 114), doesn't take sides.

¾ fl oz (20 ml) Canadian whisky	¾ fl oz (20 ml) fresh lemon juice
¾ fl oz (20 ml) Cocchi Americano	2 dashes Angostura bitters
¾ fl oz (20 ml) orange liqueur	Ice cube, for garnish

Combine the whisky, Cocchi Americano, orange liqueur, lemon juice, and bitters in a shaker, add ice, and shake hard for 8–10 seconds. Strain into a chilled coupe or cocktail glass. Garnish with the ice cube (the "iceberg").

MARY

It's ridiculous. How can it be true? Where's he been hiding for the last six years?

EDITH

In Canada, suffering from amnesia.

ROBERT

He does have a story that would explain it, but I'm not quite sure about how to test the facts.

— SEASON 2, EPISODE 6 —

COLLINS

THE VALET

MAKES **1 COCKTAIL**

Like Mr. Bates, The Valet shares its heart with Anna's variation, the Never Doubt (page 111), which also calls for Cognac and orgeat syrup. This variation on the Ramos Gin Fizz (page 47) is bolder than the original because of the orgeat, which adds more texture than nutty flavor to the morning bracer.

2 fl oz (60 ml) Cognac	4 drops orange flower water
½ fl oz (15 ml) fresh orange juice	1 egg white
½ fl oz (15 ml) fresh lemon juice	1 fl oz (30 ml) light cream (see note, page 111)
½ fl oz (15 ml) orgeat syrup	2 fl oz (60 ml) club soda

Combine the Cognac, citrus juices, orgeat syrup, orange flower water, egg white, and cream in a shaker. Add ice and shake hard for 3 minutes—or for as long as you can. Strain into a chilled collins glass. Add the club soda and stir briefly.

— LIBATION NOTE —

If you are concerned about the safety of using raw egg white here, or are simply planning on making lots of fizzes, buy a carton of pasteurized egg whites and use 1 fl oz (30 ml) for each drink.

THE DRAWING ROOM

GIN RICKEY

MAKES **1 COCKTAIL**

A member of the fizz family of mixed drinks, rickeys are made with a base spirit, fresh lime juice, and club soda and are garnished with a wedge of lime. This gin variation is the most popular drink in the fizz category, and it makes a very refreshing quaff while strolling the gardens on a hot summer day.

2 fl oz (60 ml) gin

1 fl oz (30 ml) fresh lime juice

5–6 fl oz (150–180 ml) club soda, chilled

Lime wedge, for garnish

Pour the gin and lime juice into an ice-filled collins glass. Add the club soda and stir briefly. Garnish with the lime wedge.

— **LIBATION NOTE** —

You'll notice this recipe uses no sweetener of any kind, making it a very dry drink that puts the focus on the spirit and little else. If it's too much, add some sweetener to make something more like the Raspberry Gin Fizz (see page 46).

OLD FASHIONED

BRANDY SHRUB

MAKES **3½ CUPS (825 ML)**

Not at all like a shrub in the modern sense (a sweet fruit vinegar to be mixed with soda water for a soft drink or with a spirit for a cocktail), this is nevertheless both fruity and fun. It is related to seventeenth- and eighteenth-century British shrubs, which were made of brandy or rum, citrus, and sugar, and it can be drunk neat by the hardcore, or used as a mixer with soda water, lemonade, or hot water to make a basic punch or cup. This version comes from Henry Craddock's *The Savoy Cocktail Book*, published in 1930.

1 pint (480 ml) brandy

Peel (in strips) and juice of 1 lemon

1 cup (240 ml) sherry

1 cup plus 2 tablespoons (225 g) sugar

Combine the brandy and lemon peel and juice in a tightly covered glass or ceramic container and let steep at room temperature for 3 days.

Strain the brandy mixture into a large jar, add the sherry and sugar, and cap tightly. Shake the jar a couple of times a day until the sugar is fully dissolved, up to 1 week. It's now ready to drink. Serve chilled in old fashioned glasses or in smaller pours in cordial or port glasses.

— LIBATION NOTE —

It's worth experimenting with mixers to work out which one suits you. Mixed with hot water, a slice of orange or lemon, and a slice of fresh ginger, this shrub also makes an excellent hot toddy for treating colds.

MOSELLE CUP

MAKES **2 COCKTAILS**

Cups were a popular mixed drink in Britain well before the advent of cocktails. They were drunk at parties and as an occasion drink, and they were also popular at picnics. Recipes tend to be vague—some wine, a spirit, and soda water over ice—so feel free to play with the amounts. This one uses Bénédictine, a French liqueur invented by a wine merchant in the late-Victorian period. He claimed it was based on a long-lost monastic manuscript, and he marketed it as a traditional health drink, with a secret recipe shrouded in mystery. It was made in Fécamp, in northern France, a town where many weary soldiers, war damaged and shell-shocked, were billeted after the armistice in 1918.

8 fl oz (240 ml) moselle or other sweet, light wine

8 fl oz (240 ml) soda water

2 fl oz (60 ml) Bénédictine

Fresh mint, borage, and/or lemon verbena sprigs and/or edible flowers, for garnish

Combine the wine, soda, and Bénédictine in a large mixing glass or a pitcher and stir well. Serve in collins glasses over ice. Decorate with the herb sprigs and/or flowers.

— LIBATION NOTE —

The garnish also flavors the drink, so it's important to use something you like (and that won't get in the way when you're drinking). Curls of orange or lemon zest or thin strips of cucumber will work as well.

COLLINS

UPSTAIRS COCKTAIL

MAKES **1 COCKTAIL**

There's no information on the Upstairs Cocktail in *The Savoy Cocktail Book*, recipe aside, but mixing up a couple of these reveals all you need to know: they are a refreshing and low-proof cocktail before dinner.

3 fl oz (90 ml) Dubonnet
½ fl oz (15 ml) fresh lemon juice

Seltzer water
Lemon twist, for garnish

Combine the Dubonnet and lemon juice in a collins glass with ice, then top off with the seltzer. Stir to mix. Express the lemon zest over the drink and drop it into the glass.

— LIBATION NOTE —

This drink would probably work fine with other fortified wine–based aperitifs or vermouths by simply adjusting the amount of seltzer you use.

ROBERT

Hello, Mama. Can I tempt you to one of these new cocktails?

VIOLET

No, no, I don't think so. They look too exciting for so early in the evening.

— SEASON 3, EPISODE 1 —

COLLINS

DONK

MAKES **1 COCKTAIL**

The two alcoholic beverages Lord Grantham loves the most are port and whisky, and this drink—fizzy and sweet with some nice acidity—manages to embrace both. It's a riff on the Upstairs Cocktail (page 122), with the whisky contributing heather, smoke, and turf, for contrast and depth.

½ fl oz (15 ml) fresh lemon juice
3 fl oz (90 ml) ruby port
Seltzer water

1½ barspoons peaty
Scotch whisky
Lemon twist, for garnish

Combine the lemon juice and port in a collins glass with ice, then top off with the seltzer. Stir to mix. Float the whisky on top (see note, page 75). Express the zest over the drink and drop it into the glass.

— LIBATION NOTE —

The trivial amount of whisky may seem unnecessary, but it adds depth and aroma to the cocktail. Just don't stir the drink after adding the whisky.

KNICKERBOCKER

MAKES **1 COCKTAIL**

This refreshing cocktail from the late nineteenth century drinks like a
proto-daiquiri (page 57), with just a hint of raspberry.

2 fl oz (60 ml) aged rum
½ fl oz (15 ml) fresh lime juice
1 barspoon raspberry syrup

1 barspoon curaçao
Seasonal berries, for garnish

Combine the rum, lime juice, raspberry syrup, and curaçao in a shaker.
Add ice, shake hard for 8–10 seconds, and strain into an old fashioned glass.
Garnish with the berries.

— LIBATION NOTE —

This makes for a very dry drink, so if you need something a little sweeter,
add about ½ fl oz (15 ml) more raspberry syrup.

COUPE

BIJOU

MAKES **1 COCKTAIL**

First printed in the 1900 edition of Harry Johnson's *The New and Improved Illustrated Bartenders' Manual,* the Bijou is named for the French word for "jewel," which is perhaps overselling the drink's appearance. But this classic cocktail from the German-born American bartender is both simple and delicious. The book contains a comprehensive list of rules and regulations for running a bar, like the proper temperature to keep bitters, cordials, and syrups (room temp), plus recipes and advice in both English and German.

1 fl oz (30 ml) Plymouth gin	**Dash orange bitters**
1 fl oz (30 ml) green Chartreuse	**Cherry and lemon twist,**
1 fl oz (30 ml) sweet vermouth	**for garnish**

Combine the gin, Chartreuse, vermouth, and bitters in a mixing glass filled with ice and stir until well chilled, 20–30 seconds. Strain into a chilled coupe or cocktail glass. Garnish with the cherry, putting it directly into the glass, and then express the lemon zest over the drink and drop it into the glass.

— LIBATION NOTE —

Plymouth gin is both a brand and a style of gin made in the port city of Plymouth, in the southwest of England. A regional product that differs from standard London Dry gin, Plymouth gin is earthier, with less citrus, more roots, and lighter juniper flavor.

{Reggie's letter to Matthew}

I have few intimates, and so I've decided in her name, to add you to my list of heirs. I think it unlikely that I'll outlive both the first two, so there is little chance of your reading this letter, but if you do, and if the money has come to you, know it is with my full knowledge of what transpired.

Please do not allow any grief, guilt or regret to hold you back in its employment.

God bless you, my boy,
Reggie

— SEASON 3, EPISODE 3 —

COUPE

REGGIE'S LETTER

MAKES **1 COCKTAIL**

Poor, sweet Lavinia Swire gets caught in the middle of Mary and
Matthew's destiny, much like how the sweet vermouth lands between the
gin and the Chartreuse in the Bijou (page 127). Here, swapping it out for
dry vermouth tones down the sweetness of the cocktail and gives it an
herbal note that is both refreshing and elegant.

1 fl oz (30 ml) Plymouth gin
1 fl oz (30 ml) green Chartreuse
1 fl oz (30 ml) dry vermouth
Dash orange bitters

Cherry and lemon twist,
for garnish
½ barspoon Fernet-Branca

Combine the gin, Chartreuse, vermouth, and bitters in a mixing glass filled
with ice and stir until well chilled, 20–30 seconds. Strain into a chilled coupe
or cocktail glass. Garnish with the cherry, putting it directly into the glass, and
then express the lemon zest over the drink and drop it into the glass. Float
the Fernet on top (see note, page 75).

— LIBATION NOTE —

If you carefully layer the Fernet on the surface of the cocktail,
the amaro will float on top like a dark cloud, much like this letter (see left)
to Matthew from Reggie Swire did. Thankfully, the cocktail
doesn't taste like guilt or regret.

5

THE VILLAGE

Everyday Drinks

GINGER BEER

MAKES **7 PINTS (3.3 L)**

Ginger beer was a staple drink at fetes and fairs in the 1910s and 1920s. A favorite for the servants and the family alike, it was cheap to make, easy to keep, and refreshing to drink. We see it at nearly every village occasion on *Downton*, but also at more intimate settings, such as Harold Levinson's picnic with Madeleine Allsopp in season 4. This recipe was originally published in *The Field*, Britain's premier outdoor sports and country magazine.

3½ quarts (3.3 l) water
2½ tablespoons sugar
3 tablespoons ground ginger

Peel (coarsely grated or chopped) and juice of ½ lemon
1 teaspoon active dry yeast
1 small, thick slice yeast-risen white bread, toasted

Combine the water and sugar in a large saucepan and bring to a boil over high heat. Let cool to room temperature. Add the ginger and lemon peel and juice and stir to dissolve the ginger.

In a small bowl, stir together the yeast with just enough water to make a spreadable paste and spread the paste onto the toasted bread. Put the toast into the ginger mixture, then pour the ginger mixture into a bucket or large bowl and cover with a cloth. Leave at room temperature for 24 hours. Strain the mixture through a fine-mesh sieve. Rinse out the bucket or bowl, return the strained mixture to it, and re-cover it. Leave at room temperature for 4–5 days longer.

Strain it once again, this time more carefully, using a fine-mesh sieve lined with several sheets of paper towel. Pour into clip-top bottles, which will allow you to lessen the pressure if too much builds up. The beer is ready to drink immediately.

VIOLET

You are quite wonderful, the way you see room for improvement
wherever you look. I never knew such reforming zeal.

ISOBEL

I take that as a compliment.

VIOLET

I must have said it wrong.

— SEASON 1, EPISODE 5 —

COLLINS

IMPROVED
GINGER BEER

MAKES **4 PINTS (2 L)**

A modern, easy take on ginger beer, this recipe requires minimal work and creates a flavorful drink—the perfect replacement for ginger ale. To spike a batch of ginger beer to serve bucks to your friends, add 2½ cups (600 ml) of your favorite spirit to the pitcher and stir well.

FOR THE GINGER SYRUP

3 oz (90 g) fresh ginger (about the size of a large finger)

1 cup (200 g) sugar

½ cup (120 ml) water

2 pinches of salt

FOR THE GINGER BEER

6½ cups (1.5 l) club soda, chilled

½ cup (120 ml) fresh lime juice

Lime wheels, for garnish

To make the ginger syrup, put the ginger into a fine-mesh sieve set over a small jam or Mason jar. Using a small rubber spatula or your hand, press against the solids to extract as much liquid as possible. Cover and refrigerate the juice. Reserve the ginger solids.

Combine the sugar and water in a small saucepan over medium heat and bring to a boil, stirring to dissolve the sugar. Reduce the heat, stir in the salt and ginger solids, and simmer, stirring occasionally, for 5 minutes. Remove from the heat, cover, and let cool to room temperature.

Strain the syrup through the fine-mesh sieve set over the jar holding the ginger juice, pressing against the solids once again. Cover the jar tightly and shake well. You should have 1 cup (240 ml) syrup; it will keep refrigerated for up to 1 month. To make the ginger beer, combine the club soda, lime juice, and the ginger syrup in a pitcher and stir to mix well. Serve in a collins glass over ice, garnished with a lime wheel.

BLACK VELVET

MAKES **1 COCKTAIL**

This unlikely but elegant mixture of stout and sparkling wine was developed at Brooks's Club in London in 1861, to mourn the death of Prince Albert, Queen Victoria's prince consort. It is meant to symbolize the black band worn during mourning.

6 fl oz (180 ml) Irish stout, chilled

6 fl oz (180 ml) Champagne or sparkling wine, chilled

Carefully pour the stout and Champagne into a chilled pint glass or wineglass.

— **LIBATION NOTE** —

Sweeter sparkling wines work best here. If you're using dry sparkling wine, like a brut, add up to ½ fl oz (15 ml) simple syrup (see note, page 37) to the drink to help the flavors meld.

COUPE

ROB ROY

MAKES **1 COCKTAIL**

A twist on the Manhattan (page 147), the Rob Roy is said to have originated in 1894 at New York's Waldorf-Astoria hotel. Its inspiration was the Manhattan premiere of an operetta about the life of Rob Roy MacGregor, known as the Scottish Robin Hood.

2 fl oz (60 ml) blended Scotch whisky

1 fl oz (30 ml) sweet vermouth

2 dashes Angostura or other aromatic bitters

2 cherries, for garnish

Combine the whisky, vermouth, and bitters in a mixing glass filled with ice and stir until well chilled, 20–30 seconds. Strain into a chilled coupe or cocktail glass. Garnish with the cherries pieced together with a cocktail pick.

— LIBATION NOTE —

Try adding a float of peaty whisky on top (see note, page 75) for some additional complexity.

PINT GLASS

BLOODY MARY

MAKES **1 COCKTAIL**

Bartender Fernand Petiot reportedly created this classic in the 1920s at Harry's New York Bar in Paris, an American-style bar owned at the time by a former well-known American jockey, Tod Sloan. It has changed greatly over the years, and everyone seems to have a favorite take calling for an extra pinch of one seasoning or another. This recipe is basic but well balanced.

2 fl oz (60 ml) vodka

4 fl oz (120 ml) tomato juice

½ fl oz (15 ml) fresh lime juice

¼ barspoon black pepper

¼ barspoon ground cumin

Generous pinch of salt

2 dashes Worcestershire sauce

2 dashes hot sauce

Lime wedge, for garnish

Celery stalk, for garnish

Combine the vodka, tomato juice, lime juice, pepper, cumin, salt, Worcestershire sauce, and hot sauce in a shaker with ice and shake hard for 8–10 seconds. Pour the mixture, ice and all, into a pint glass. Garnish with the lime wedge and celery.

LIBATION NOTE

You can make up a batch of
Bloody Marys the night before
you plan to serve them, mixing
together everything but the lime
juice and garnishes and skipping
the ice. Refrigerate in a tightly
capped container. The next day,
add the lime juice and serve over
ice. Feel free to go crazy with the
garnishes, which can turn this
drink from hangover helper into
a full meal.

STOUT SANGAREE

MAKES **1 COCKTAIL**

Here is a hearty drink perfect for enjoying near the fireplace at the pub. It is part of the sangaree category of mixed drinks, whose members are all made with a base wine, spirit, or beer and a sweetening agent. In this version, ruby port adds sweetness and brightness to the mix. Sangarees (whose name is a variant of sangria) can be served over ice, neat, or straight up in a wineglass or beer glass.

1¼ cups (300 ml) Irish stout
3 fl oz (90 ml) ruby port

Ground or freshly grated nutmeg, for garnish

Pour the stout and port into a large wineglass. Sprinkle with the nutmeg.

— LIBATION NOTE —

If you suddenly find yourself living upstairs, replace the ruby port with tawny port, which is aged longer, so it oxidizes slightly and has a deeper, more complex flavor. But scale back the amount of stout to let the flavors of the port shine.

COLLINS

ORANGEADE

MAKES ¾ CUP (180 ML)

This orange syrup works great as a mixer, but it is just as good diluted with club soda as a refreshing nonalcoholic drink (see note). It calls for an old English technique in which sugar is used to extract the essential oils and flavor from citrus peel to create *oleo saccharum* (oil sugar).

1 orange

¼ cup (50 g) sugar

½ cup (120 ml) fresh orange juice, strained

¼ cup (60 ml) fresh lemon juice, strained

½ barspoon orange flower water

Using a vegetable peeler, remove the zest from the orange in wide strips and combine it with the sugar in a Mason jar. Using a wooden muddler or a wooden spoon, lightly mash together the zest and sugar. Cover the jar with a lid and let sit at room temperature for 24 hours, until the sugar is fully moistened and liquid has formed. Strain the mixture through a fine-mesh sieve, pressing against the solids to extract as much liquid as possible. Discard the zest.

Add the orange juice, lemon juice, and orange flower water to the zest-sugar liquid and stir to combine. It is best if the syrup is used right away, but it will keep in an airtight container in the refrigerator for up to 5 days.

> — LIBATION NOTE —
>
> To mix as a beverage, combine ¼ cup (60 ml) of the syrup with ¾ cup (180 ml) club soda in a collins glass filled with ice and stir briefly.

COUPE

BOBBY BURNS

MAKES **1 COCKTAIL**

The Bobby Burns is a simple variation on the Rob Roy (page 137), dressed up with the addition of a little Bénédictine. The herbal liqueur became popular in England after World War I, particularly in the Burnley area, when injured soldiers from the East Lancashire Regiment developed a taste for it while recuperating at the Bénédictine distillery-turned-makeshift-hospital.

2 fl oz (60 ml) blended Scotch whisky

1 fl oz (30 ml) sweet vermouth

2 dashes Angostura or other

aromatic bitters

1 barspoon Bénédictine, or ½ barspoon absinthe

2 cherries, for garnish

Combine the whisky, vermouth, bitters, and Bénédictine in a mixing glass filled with ice and stir until well chilled, 20–30 seconds. Strain into a chilled coupe or cocktail glass. Garnish with the cherries pieced together with a cocktail pick.

– LIBATION NOTE –

There are two versions of this drink, one from *The Savoy Cocktail Book* that calls for Bénédictine and one from the Waldorf-Astoria that uses ½ barspoon absinthe. The difference is slight but distinct. The absinthe makes the drink light and bright, while the Bénédictine version leans toward chocolate and dark fruit.

MUG

TOM AND JERRY

SERVES **24**

During the cold season, this early-nineteenth-century drink will warm you up. Although it is traditionally served from a Tom and Jerry bowl into Tom and Jerry cups, any bowl and mugs will work. Don't beat the egg whites here to stiff peaks. All you need to add to the batter is some volume. You don't need structure, like you would for a meringue.

12 eggs, separated

1½ cups (300 g) sugar

1 teaspoon baking soda

2 cups (480 ml) dark rum

2 cups (480 ml) brandy

2 quarts plus 1 cup (2.1 l) whole milk, scalded

Ground or freshly grated nutmeg, for garnish

In a large bowl, combine the egg yolks, 1¼ cups (250 g) of the sugar, and the baking soda and whisk until the mixture is thick and creamy.

In a Tom and Jerry bowl or other large bowl, using a handheld mixer on medium speed, beat the egg whites until frothy. Sprinkle in the remaining ¼ cup (50 g) sugar, raise the speed to medium-high, and beat until soft peaks form. Using a rubber spatula, fold the egg whites into the egg yolk mixture just until combined, forming a thick batter.

Whisking constantly, gradually add the rum and brandy to the batter.

Divide the batter evenly among 24 Tom and Jerry cups or heatproof punch cups (each should hold about ¾ cup/180 ml). Add about ⅓ cup (80 ml) hot milk to each cup (just pour it in, don't stir). Sprinkle the nutmeg over each serving.

OLD FASHIONED

MAKES **1 COCKTAIL**

If there were a First Earl and Countess of Grantham of cocktails, this would be it. The drink is an evolution of the sling, one of the earliest cocktails that simply combined spirits with water and sweetener. Adding bitters made it what today we know as an old fashioned. In the nineteenth century it was known as a bittered sling; calling it an old fashioned came later, when the drink was, by that time, old-fashioned.

1 sugar cube, ¾ barspoon granulated sugar, or 1 barspoon gum syrup

2 dashes bitters (usually Angostura)

1 large ice cube

2 fl oz (60 ml) whiskey

Lemon twist, for garnish

Put the sugar into an old fashioned or rocks glass, then add the bitters and a couple of dashes of water—just enough to moisten the sugar. Using a muddler, crush the sugar, dissolving it as much as possible. Add the ice cube and the whiskey and give everything a stir with a barspoon. Express the lemon zest over the drink and drop it into the glass.

— LIBATION NOTE —

This formula works with almost any unsweetened spirit and almost any sweetener, along with any bitters. It's the perfect prescription for experimenting to find what you like best.

COCKTAIL

MANHATTAN

MAKES **1 COCKTAIL**

The origins of the Manhattan are disputed, but the drink was developed sometime in the 1860s. It shows up in the 1887 edition of Jerry Thomas's *The Bar-Tenders Guide*, with the addition of a liqueur (Thomas suggests either curaçao or maraschino).

2 fl oz (60 ml) rye whiskey or a high-rye Canadian whisky	**2 dashes Angostura bitters**
1 fl oz (30 ml) sweet vermouth	**2 cherries, for garnish**

Combine the whiskey, vermouth, and bitters in a mixing glass filled with ice and stir until well chilled, 20–30 seconds. Strain into a chilled cocktail glass or coupe. Garnish with the cherries pieced together with a cocktail pick.

— **LIBATION NOTE** —

Originally made with rye whiskey, this recipe is the framework for other cocktails, including The Boothby (page 96), the Rob Roy (page 137), and the Bobby Burns (page 143).

DRY MARTINI

MAKES **1 COCKTAIL**

The classic and most famous of the cocktails, with a ratio of two parts gin to one part dry vermouth, is still one of the most elegant and sophisticated drinks around. While the gin is important, the vermouth is perhaps the most critical component. For silky martinis, keep your vermouth fresh and store it in the fridge.

2 fl oz (60 ml) gin
1 fl oz (30 ml) dry vermouth

Green cocktail olives or lemon twist, for garnish

Combine the gin and vermouth in a mixing glass filled with ice and stir until well chilled, 20–30 seconds. Strain into a chilled cocktail glass or coupe. Add the olives, pieced together with a cocktail pick if desired. If garnishing with a lemon twist, express the lemon zest over the drink and drop it into the glass.

— LIBATION NOTE —

If you enjoy your martinis with a lemon twist, try adding ½ fl oz (15 ml) blanc or bianco vermouth, which is sweeter, along with the dry vermouth.

TOM COLLINS

MAKES **1 COCKTAIL**

This drink is believed to be a variation on the John Collins (page 62), made with Old Tom gin instead of genever. That makes sense, given that genever is sweetened with malt wine and Old Tom is a sweetened gin. Here we stick with the modern interpretation, using London Dry gin and a hit of simple syrup.

2 fl oz (60 ml) London Dry gin	5–6 fl oz (150–180 ml) club soda
½ fl oz (15 ml) fresh lemon juice	Lemon wedge, for garnish
½ fl oz (15 ml) simple syrup (see note, page 37)	

Combine the gin, lemon juice, and simple syrup in a shaker. Add ice, shake hard for 8–10 seconds, and strain into a collins glass filled with ice. Pour in the club soda and stir briefly. Garnish with the lemon wedge.

> — LIBATION NOTE —
>
> If you want to try it with Old Tom gin, just be aware that the Old Tom is sweeter than the standard London Dry varieties, so depending on the brand of gin, you may need to adjust the amount of simple syrup.

HOT BUTTERED RUM

MAKES **1 COCKTAIL**

This sweet, spice-laced, spiked beverage—also known as a hot toddy—
has its origin in colonial America, where New England distillers were
turning molasses imported from Jamaica into rum as early as the 1650s.
The steaming-hot mix of the strong local spirit and rich butter provided
a welcome defense against the bitter-cold Northeast winter. Don't be
tempted to stir the melted butter into the drink. It should float on top.

2 fl oz (60 ml) dark rum

**½ fl oz (15 ml) simple syrup
(see note, page 37)**

3 whole cloves

**1 cinnamon stick, about
3 inches (7.5 cm) long**

**½–⅔ cup (120–160 ml)
boiling water**

**1 barspoon (about 1 pat)
unsalted butter (see note)**

**Ground or freshly grated
nutmeg, for garnish**

Pour the rum and simple syrup into a heatproof mug or an Irish coffee glass.
Add the cloves and the cinnamon stick. Pour in the boiling water almost to
fill the glass. Float the butter on top (so it will melt slowly), then sprinkle
with the nutmeg.

— **LIBATION NOTE** —

Salted butter works well here, too, adding just enough salinity
to brighten up the rum and spices.

APPLE
HOT TODDY

MAKES **1 COCKTAIL**

Adapted from one of the oldest cocktail recipes, this version omits the mashing of the apple into the drink, drawing a majority of its apple flavor from the brandy instead. Feel free to mash the apple into the drink if you'd prefer. If you opt for tradition, keep the peel on, as it contains a good deal of the aroma and flavor of the fruit.

3 barspoons (½ oz/15 g) sugar

Boiling water, as needed

**2 fl oz (60 ml) Calvados
or other apple brandy**

¼ baked apple

**Whole nutmeg,
for garnish**

In a large heatproof mug, combine the sugar and a small amount of boiling water and stir until the sugar dissolves. Pour in the brandy and enough boiling water to fill the mug and stir well. Add the baked apple and grate a little nutmeg on top.

INDEX

A

The Abbey, 48
Absinthe
  Bobby Burns, 143
  Clarkson's Antidote, 113
  Corpse Reviver No. 2, 114
  Green Swizzle, 56
  Improved Brandy Cocktail, 36
  London Cocktail, 24
  Morning Coat, 35
  Tuxedo Cocktail No.2, 32
Apple brandy
  Apple Hot Toddy, 153
  Clarkson's Antidote, 113
  Corpse Reviver No. 1, 112
Archie's Memorial, 92

B

Baltimore Eggnog, 31
Bénédictine
  Bobby Burns, 143
  Moselle Cup, 121
Bijou, 127
Black Velvet, 136
Bloody Mary, 138
Bobby Burns, 143
The Boothby, 96
Bosom Caresser, 23
The Boulevardier, 28
Bourbon
  The Boulevardier, 28
  Mint Julep, 60
Brandy. See also Apple brandy
  Bosom Caresser, 23
  Brandy Crusta, 83
  Brandy Shrub, 120
  Coffee Cocktail, 37
  Fish House Punch, 101
  Prince of Wales Punch, 102
  Sidecar, 43
  The Suffragette, 44
  Tea Punch, 79
  Tom and Jerry, 144
  Turkish Attaché, 83

C

Campari
  The Boulevardier, 28
  The Cheerful Charlies, 17
  Lady's Maid, 77
  Old Pal, 14
Canadian whisky
  The Boothby, 96
  The Cheerful Charlies, 17
  Manhattan, 147

Old Pal, 14
Petrick, 116
Champagne
  Black Velvet, 136
  Champagne Cobbler, 67
  Kir Royal, 93
  Prince of Wales Punch, 102
Chartreuse
  Bijou, 127
  Last Word, 68
  Reggie's Letter, 129
The Cheerful Charlies, 17
Clarkson's Antidote, 113
Clover Club, 59
Cocchi Americano
  The Abbey, 48
  Corpse Reviver No. 2, 114
  Downton Heir, 51
  Marigold, 21
  Morning Coat, 35
  Petrick, 116
Coffee Cocktail, 37
Cognac
  Baltimore Eggnog, 31
  The Cheerful Charlies, 17
  Corpse Reviver No. 1, 112
  Daisy, 63
  Improved Brandy Cocktail, 36
  Japanese Cocktail, 29
  Mason Daisy, 65
  Metropole, 22
  Never Doubt, 111
  The Valet, 117
Corpse Reviver No. 1, 112
Corpse Reviver No. 2, 114
Crème de cacao
  Morning Glory Fizz, 108
  The Suffragette, 44
Crème de cassis
  Kir Royal, 93
  Wedding Coat, 104
Crème de violet
  Final Say, 71
Curaçao
  Bosom Caresser, 23
  Knickerbocker, 126
  Prince of Wales Punch, 102
  Stirrup Cup, 94

D, E

Daiquiri, 57
Daisy, 63
Donk, 125
Downton Heir, 51
Dry Martini, 149
Dubonnet
  Upstairs Cocktail, 122

Eggs
  Baltimore Eggnog, 31
  Bosom Caresser, 23
  Clover Club, 59
  Ramos Gin Fizz, 118
  Sherry Flip, 27
  Tom & Jerry, 144
  The Valet, 117

F

Falernum & Velvet Falernum
  Green Swizzle, 56
  Turkish Attaché, 83
Fernet & Fernet-Branca
  Hanky Panky, 18
  Marigold, 21
Final Say, 71
Fish House Punch, 101
French 75, 91

G

Genever
  John Collins, 62
  Pineapple Julep, 98
Ghillies Juice, 80
Gin
  The Abbey, 48
  Archie's Memorial, 92
  Bijou, 127
  Clover Club, 59
  Corpse Reviver No. 2, 114
  Downton Heir, 51
  Dry Martini, 149
  Final Say, 71
  French 75, 91
  Gin Rickey, 118
  Hanky Panky, 18
  Last Word, 68
  London Cocktail, 24
  Marigold, 21
  Ramos Gin Fizz, 47
  Raspberry Gin Fizz, 46
  Reggie's Letter, 129
  Tom Collins, 150
  Tuxedo Cocktail No. 2, 32
  Wedding Coat, 104
  White Lady, 103
Ginger beer
  Ginger Beer, 132
  Improved Ginger Beer, 135
  Mason Daisy, 65
  Sub-rosa Summer, 55
Green Swizzle, 56

H, I, J, K, L

Hanky Panky, 18
Hot Buttered Rum, 151
Hot Toddy, Apple, 153

Improved Brandy Cocktail, 36
Improved Ginger Beer, 135
Japanese Cocktail, 29
John Collins, 62
Kir Royal, 93
Knickerbocker, 126
Lady's Maid, 77
Last Word, 68
London Cocktail, 24

M

Madeira
  Baltimore Eggnog, 31
Manhattan, 147
Maraschino liqueur
  Final Say, 71
  Improved Brandy Cocktail, 36
  Last Word, 68
  Morning Coat, 35
  Pineapple Julep, 98
  Prince of Wales Cocktail, 87
  Stirrup Cup, 94
  Tuxedo Cocktail No.2, 32
  Wild Rose, 88
Marigold, 21
Martini, Dry, 149
Mason Daisy, 65
Metropole, 22
Mint Julep, 60
Morning Coat, 35
Morning Glory Fizz, 108
Moselle Cup, 121

N, O

Never Doubt, 111
New York Sour, 75
Old Fashioned, 146
Old Pal, 14
Orangeade, 142
Orange liqueur
  Bosom Caresser, 23
  Brandy Crusta, 83
  The Cheerful Charlies, 17
  Corpse Reviver No. 2, 114
  Daisy, 63
  Mason Daisy, 65
  Petrick, 116
  Sidecar, 43
  White Lady, 103

P

Petrick, 116
Pimm's No. 1
  Sub-rosa Summer, 55
  Summer Cup, 52
Pineapple Julep, 98
Planter's Punch, 99

Port
  Baltimore Eggnog, 31
  Donk, 125
  Lady's Maid, 77
  Stirrup Cup, 94
  Stout Sangaree, 141
Prince of Wales Cocktail, 87
Prince of Wales Punch, 102

R

Ramos Gin Fizz, 47
Raspberry Gin Fizz, 46
Reggie's Letter, 129
Rob Roy, 137
Rum
  Baltimore Eggnog, 31
  Clarkson's Antidote, 113
  Daiquiri, 57
  Fish House Punch, 101
  Green Swizzle, 56
  Hot Buttered Rum, 151
  Knickerbocker, 126
  Planter's Punch, 99
  Prince of Wales Punch, 102
  Tea Punch, 79
  Tom and Jerry, 144
Rye
  The Boothby, 96
  The Cheerful Charlies, 17
  Manhattan, 147
  Old Pal, 14
  Prince of Wales Cocktail, 87

S

Sangaree, Stout, 141
Scotch whisky
  Bobby Burns, 143
  Donk, 125
  Morning Glory Fizz, 108
  Rob Roy, 137
Sherry
  Brandy Shrub, 120
  Sherry Flip, 27
Shrub, Brandy, 120
Sidecar, 43
Sparkling wine. See also Champagne
  Archie's Memorial, 92
  Black Velvet, 136
  The Boothby, 96
  French 75, 91
  Kir Royal, 93
  Pineapple Julep, 98
  Prince of Wales Cocktail, 87
  Wild Rose, 88
Stirrup Cup, 94
Stout
  Black Velvet, 136

Stout Sangaree, 141
Sub-rosa Summer, 55
The Suffragette, 44
Summer Cup, 52

T, U

Tea
  Ghillies Juice, 80
  Tea Punch, 79
Tequila
  Wild Rose, 88
Tom Collins, 150
Tom and Jerry, 144
Turkish Attaché, 83
Tuxedo Cocktail No. 2, 32
Upstairs Cocktail, 122

V

The Valet, 117
Vermouth
  Bijou, 127
  Bobby Burns, 143
  The Boothby, 96
  The Boulevardier, 28
  The Cheerful Charlies, 17
  Clarkson's Antidote, 113
  Clover Club, 59
  Corpse Reviver No. 1, 112
  Downton Heir, 51
  Dry Martini, 149
  Hanky Panky, 18
  Manhattan, 147
  Metropole, 22
  Old Pal, 14
  Reggie's Letter, 129
  Rob Roy, 137
  Tuxedo Cocktail No. 2, 32
Vodka
  Bloody Mary, 138

W

Wedding Coat, 104
Whiskey. See also Bourbon; Rye
  Lady's Maid, 77
  Morning Coat, 35
  New York Sour, 75
  Old Fashioned, 146
Whisky. See also Canadian whisky;
Scotch whisky
  Ghillies Juice, 80
White Lady, 103
Wild Rose, 88
Wine. See also Port; Sparkling wine
  Moselle Cup, 121
  New York Sour, 75
  Prince of Wales Punch, 102

ROSE

I love cocktail parties.

CORA

Me, too. You only have to stay forty minutes, instead of
sitting for seven courses, between a deaf landowner and
an even deafer major general.

— SEASON 5, EPISODE 5 —

weldon**owen**

President & Publisher **Roger Shaw**
Associate Publisher **Amy Marr**
Creative Director **Kelly Booth**
Art Director & Designer **Lisa Berman**
Photo Shoot Art Director **Marisa Kwek**
Managing Editor **Tarji Rodriguez**
Production Manager **Binh Au**
Production Designer **Carlos Esparza**

Drinks Photographer **John Kernick**
Food Stylist **Cyd Raftus McDowell**
Prop Stylist **Suzie Myers**

Produced by Weldon Owen
1045 Sansome Street
San Francisco, CA 94111
www.weldonowen.com

Library of Congress Cataloging-in-Publication
data is available.
ISBN: 978-1-68188-998-6

Printed and bound in China
First printed in 2019
10 9 8 7 6 5 4 3 2 1

WRITTEN BY **LOU BUSTAMANTE,**
author of *The Complete Cocktail Manual*

WELDON OWEN WISHES TO THANK THE FOLLOWING PEOPLE
FOR THEIR GENEROUS SUPPORT IN PRODUCING THIS BOOK

Julian Fellowes, Rizwan Alvi, Lisa Atwood, Debbie Berne, Lesley Bruynesteyn,
Annie Gray, Rishon Hanners, Rae Hellard, Rachel Markowitz, Joan Olson, Elizabeth Parson,
Nico Sherman, Sharon Silva, Josh Simons, Angela Williams, and Tammy White

CARNIVAL FILMS Gareth Neame, Aliboo Bradbury, Charlotte Fay, and Nion Hazell
NBCUNIVERSAL Dominic Burns
PETERS FRASER + DUNLOP Annabel Merullo and Laura McNeill
CUMBRIA CRYSTAL Chris Blade, Beverley Frankland, Carole Garnett, and Craig Hill
IMAGINE EXHIBITIONS Jay Hering, Jeffrey Millar, Whitney Sinkule, and Vince Quarta
HARROGATE TIPPLE Steven Green